Photos from the Cell Phone

Photos may not be used without permission.

ISBN-13: 978-1497401013
ISBN-10: 1497401011

Dedicated to the ones who followed my Instagram photos on Facebook.

Contents

Introduction

I enjoy challenges. The iPhone 4 introduced a huge one for me. Unlike most cameras, the iPhone's camera possessed no optical zoom. Optical zoom is a true zoom. Digital zoom, something the phone did have, is a fake zoom. Unlike optical, digital zoom crops within the image. Do enough of that and a messy image appears. So, what did I use for zoom instead? My two feet. I moved as close to the image as possible.

Also, iPhone 4 owns a terrible flash. Most times, I wound up with redeye images. Instead, when it involved people, I attempted using the light already available.

The third challenge traveled me back to the 1970s and 1980s, the childhood and teen years I saw square shaped photos. Instagram only allows square shaped photos. So, in order to gain the perfect shot for Instagram, I worked within a square on the phone. (For those who don't know what Instagram is, welcome to the 21st Century.)

After photographing, I used phone apps like Photoshop Express and Snapseed. Most of the times, I used Snapseed. Next, I uploaded the photo to Instagram for one more edit. Usually, this involved adding the lo-fi filter to the photo.

The best thing I loved about it? Everything, including the phone apps, was free.

Next, the unexpected part arrived. I also uploaded photos to Facebook, Tumblr and Twitter. I didn't expect Facebook friends to enjoy the photos. At least, I didn't expect to gain somewhat of a following for them.

Many times, when I run into friends, they tell me they enjoy the Instagram photos I post on Facebook. When professional photographers told me this, shock slapped me silly. I couldn't believe it. Professional photographers complemented my phone pics. PHONE PICS!!!

The following content separates by city and sections. All photographs involve Central Florida.

In parenthesis, I sometimes indicate the subject's location.

Now, I present my photographs.

1.
Around the House

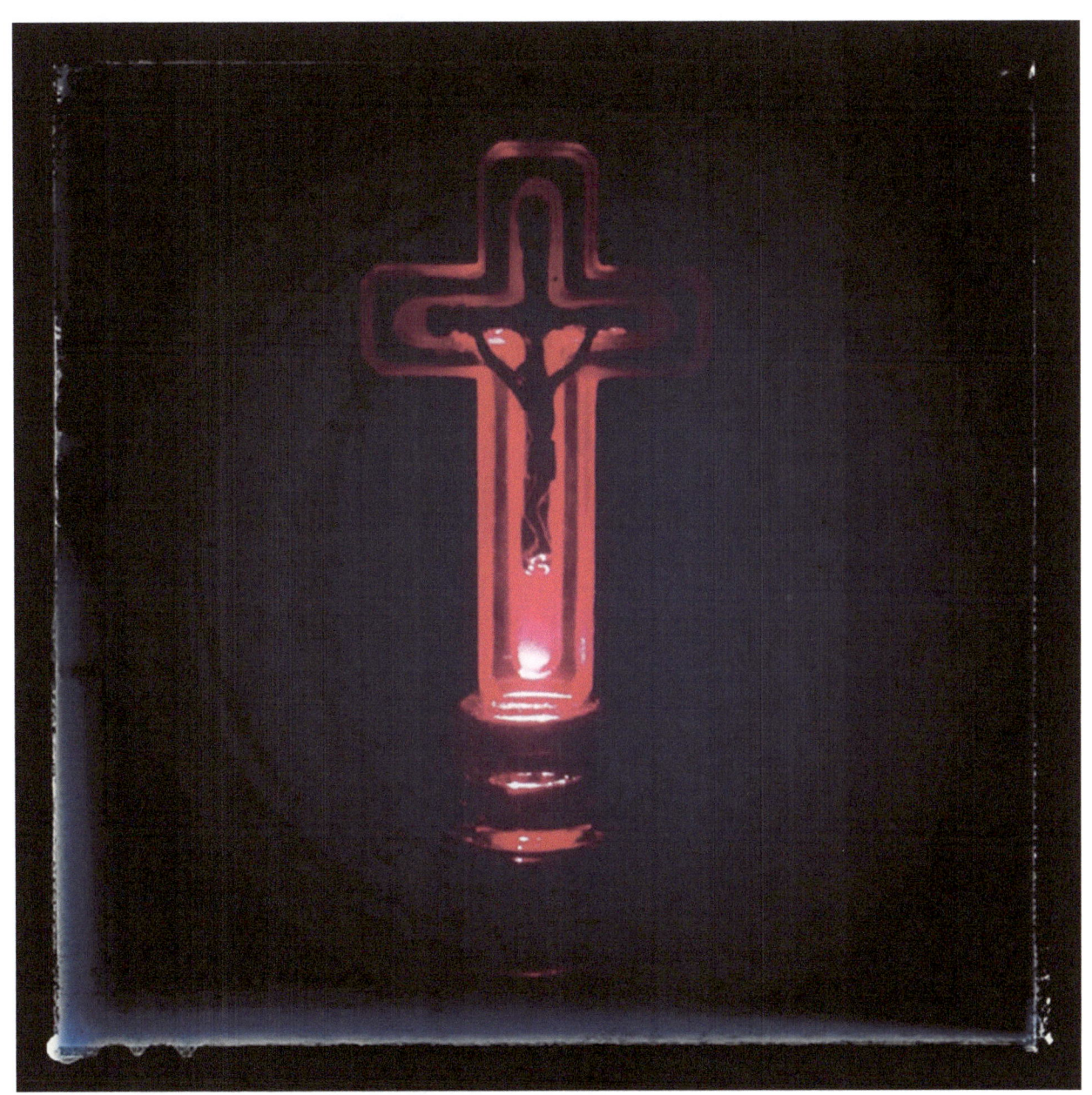

Crucifixion

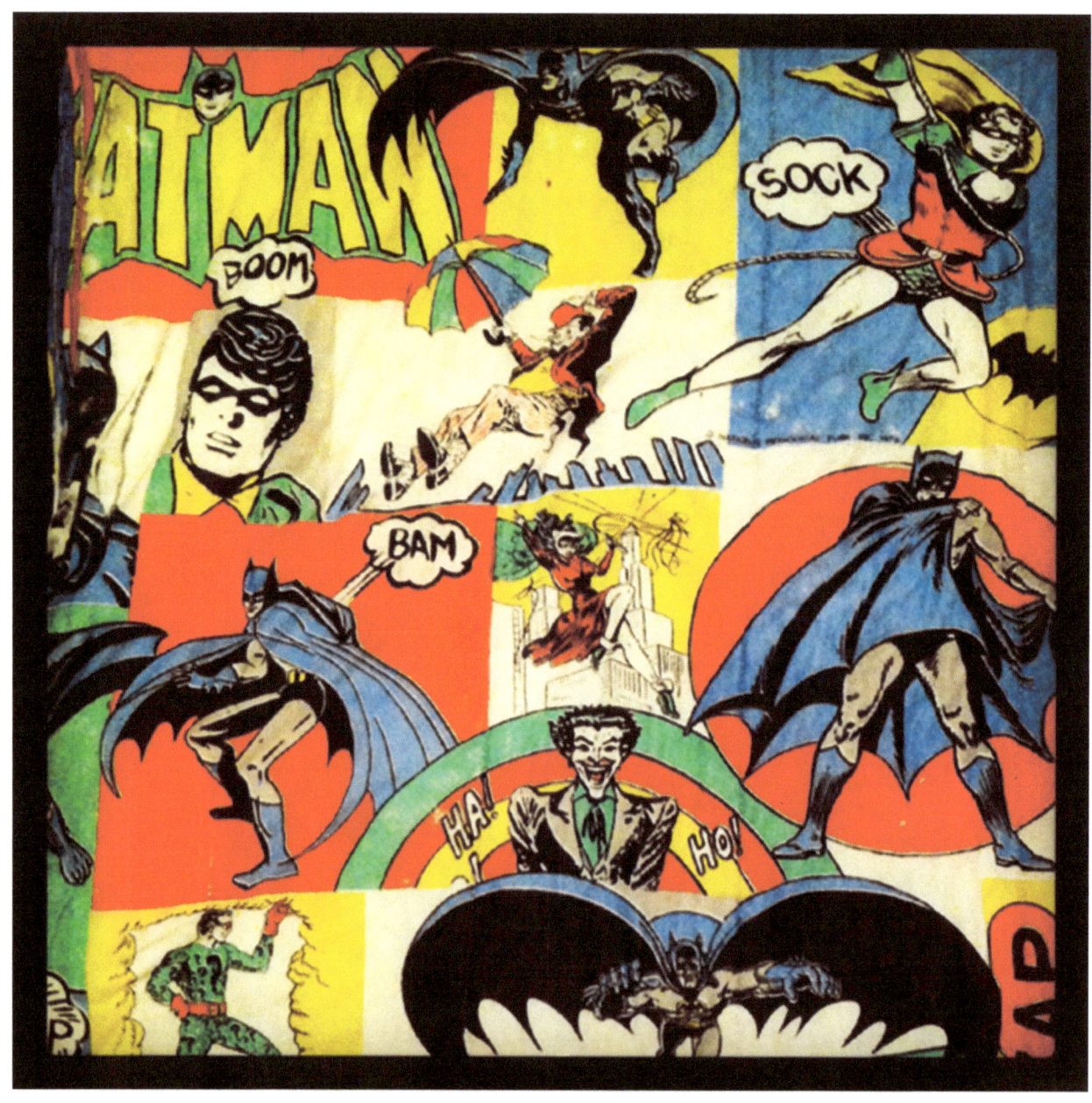

Batman Sleeping Bag
1970s Christmas Present from Grandma Eva

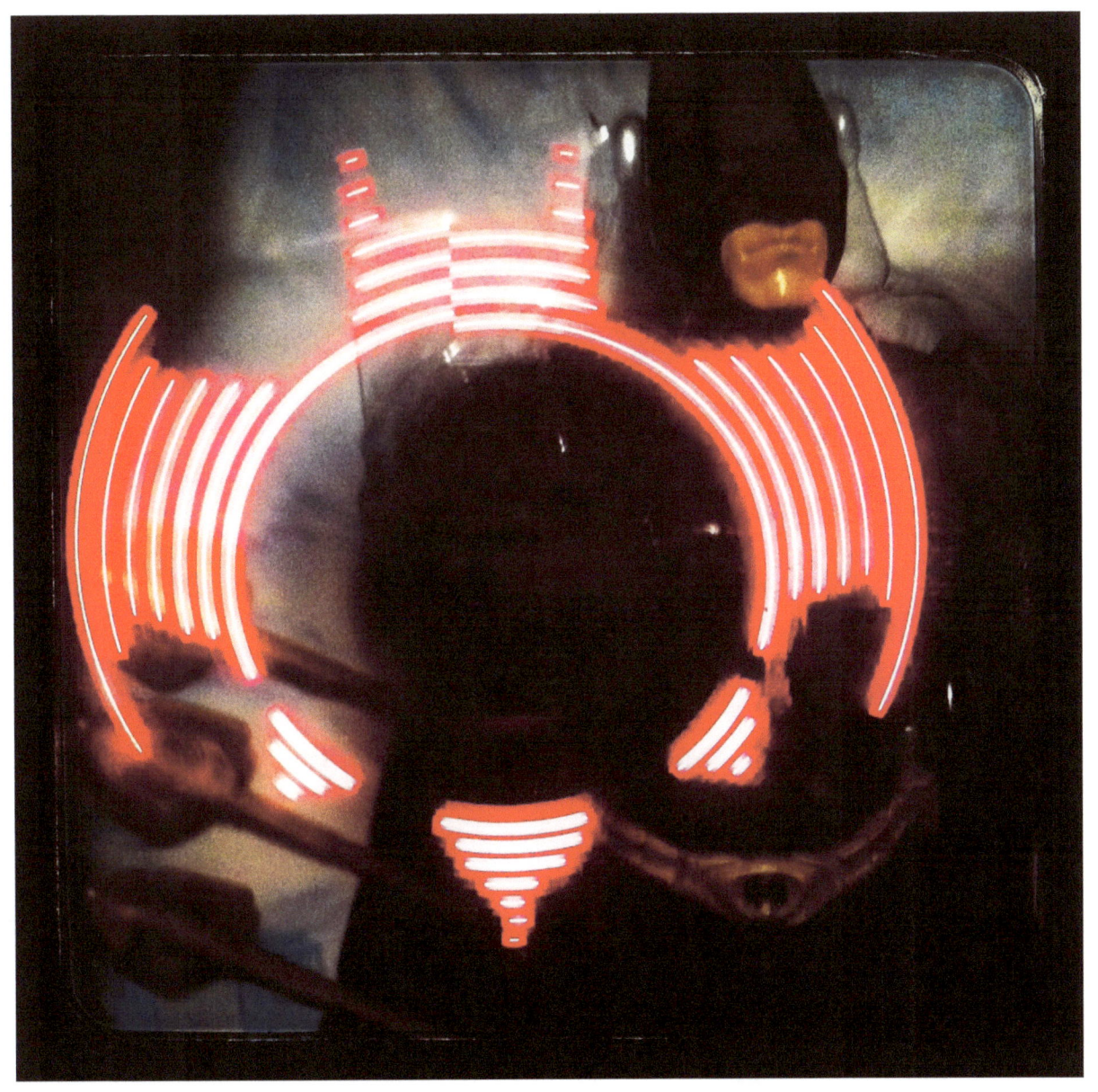

Stealth Signal Batman
2000s Birthday Present from my Friend Jim

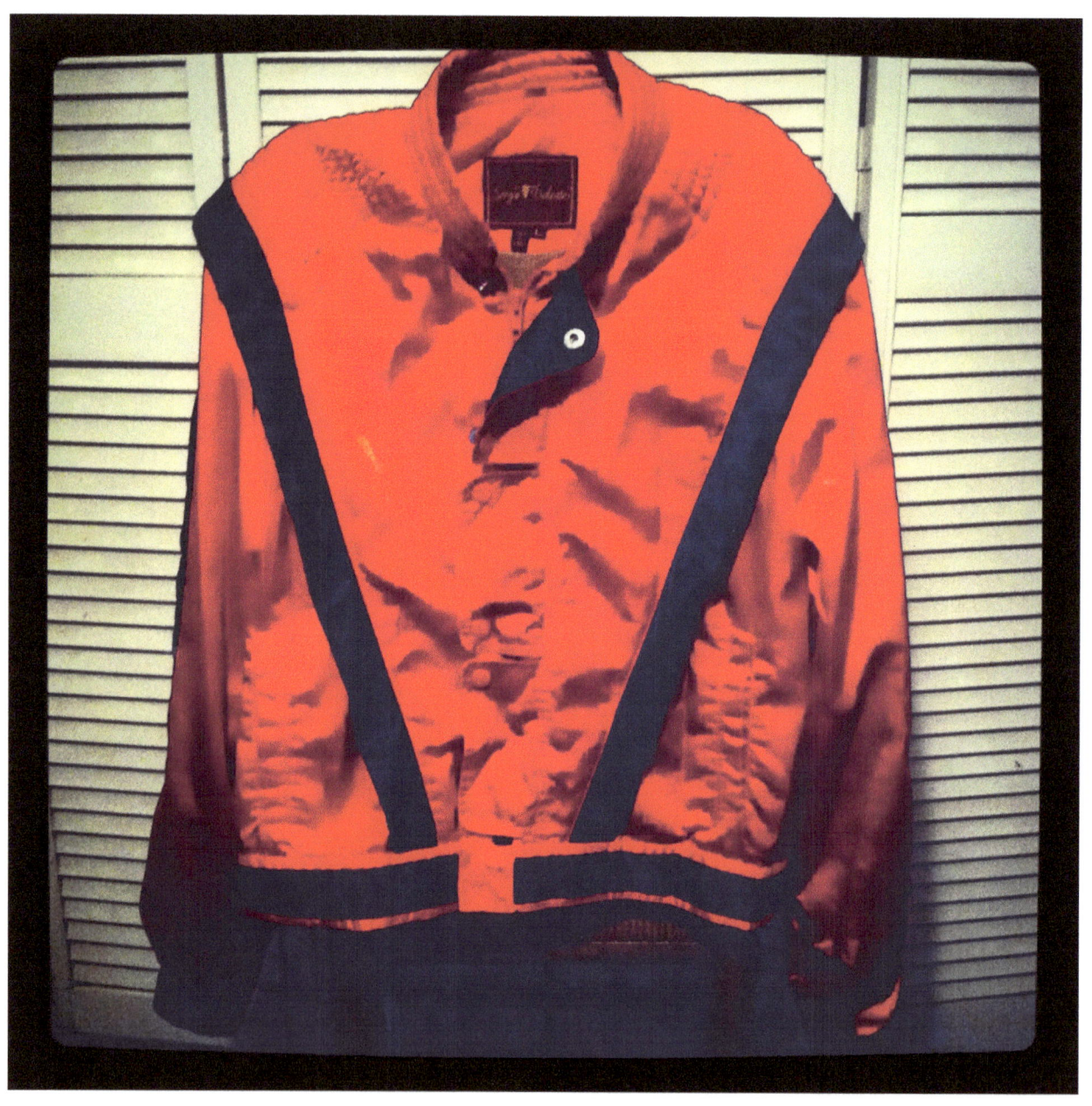

Nylon Version of Michael Jackson's Thriller Jacket

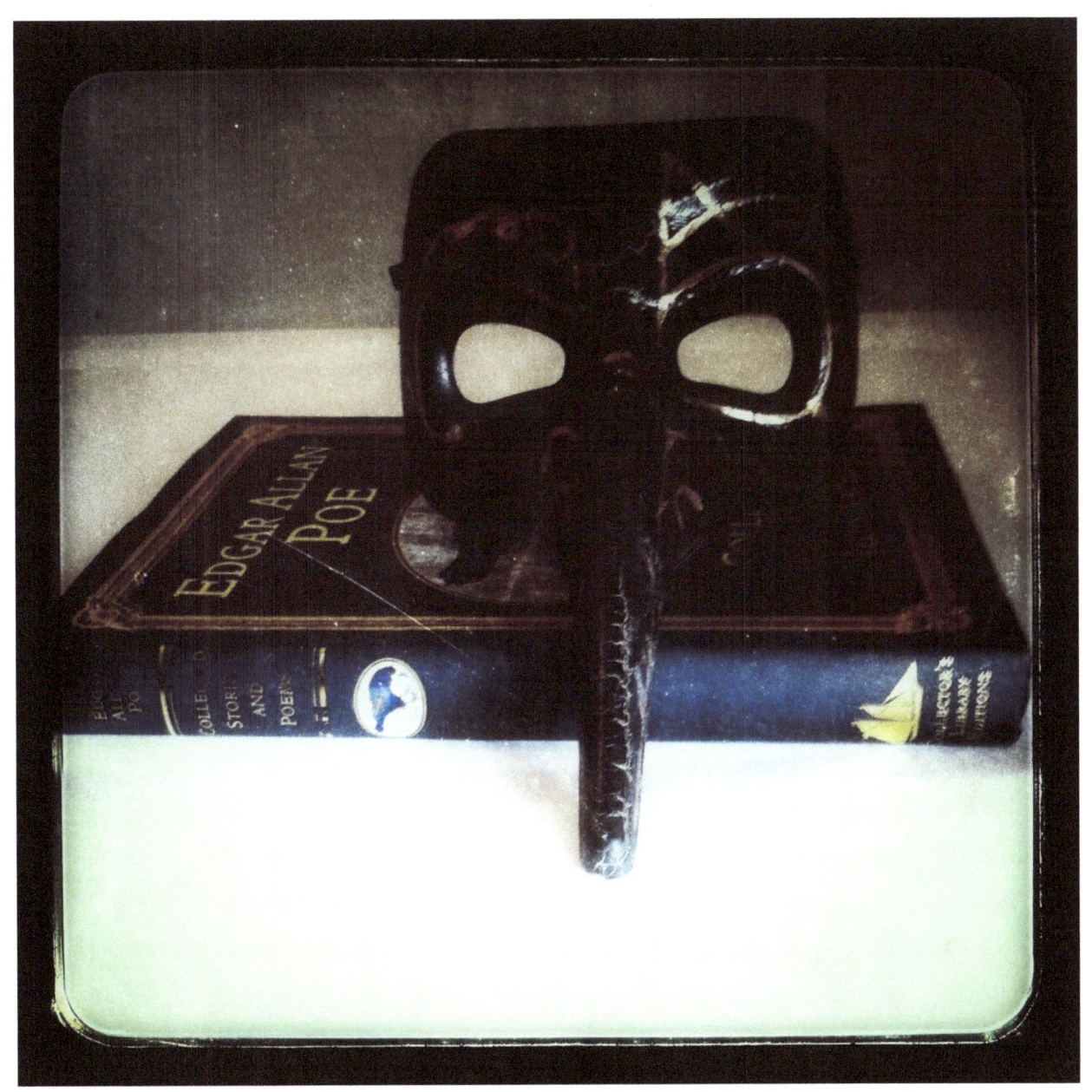

Mask and Book

2.
Altamonte Springs, Florida

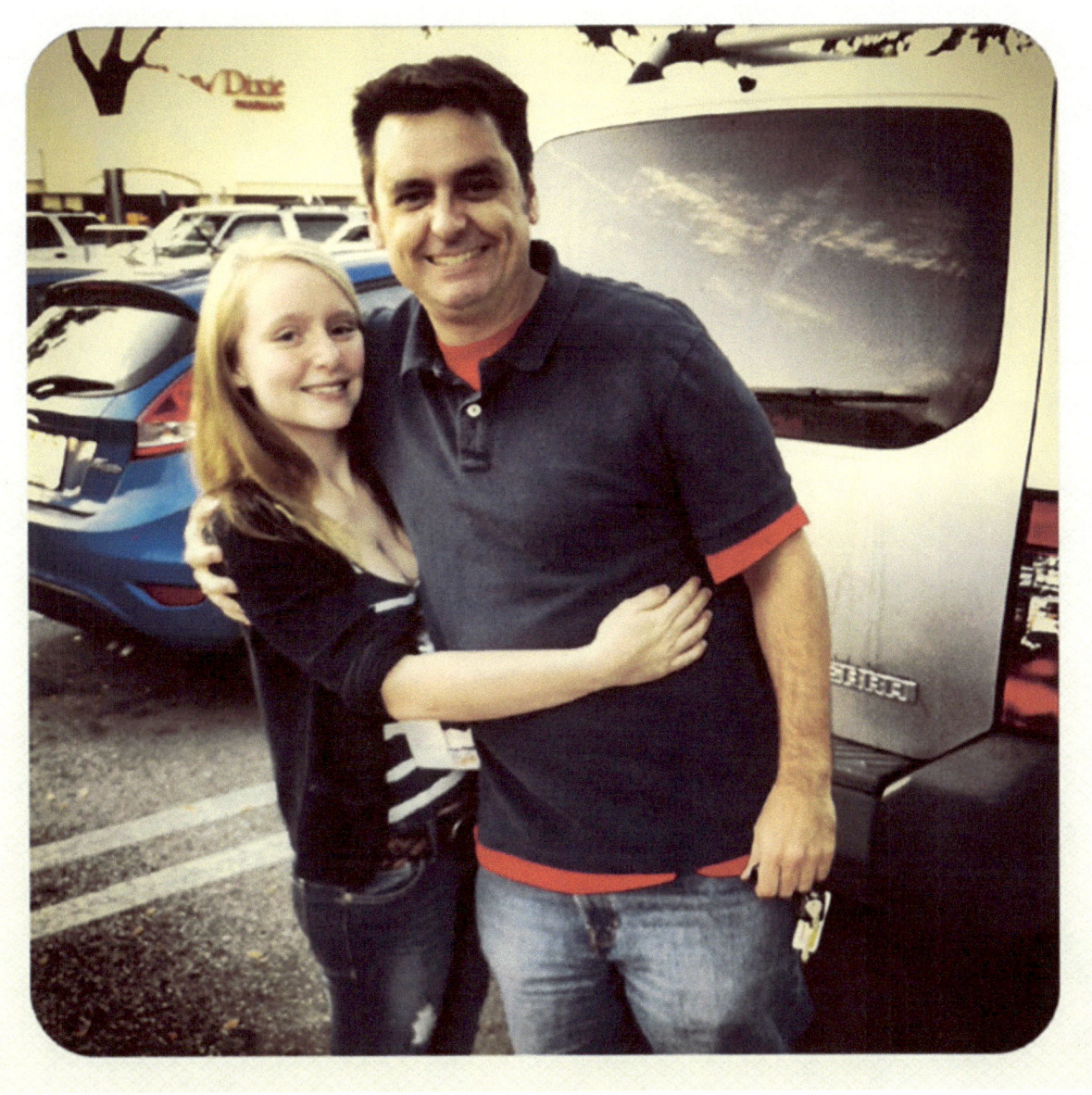

Mike Piazza and Daughter Rhi
(Winn Dixie Parking Lot)

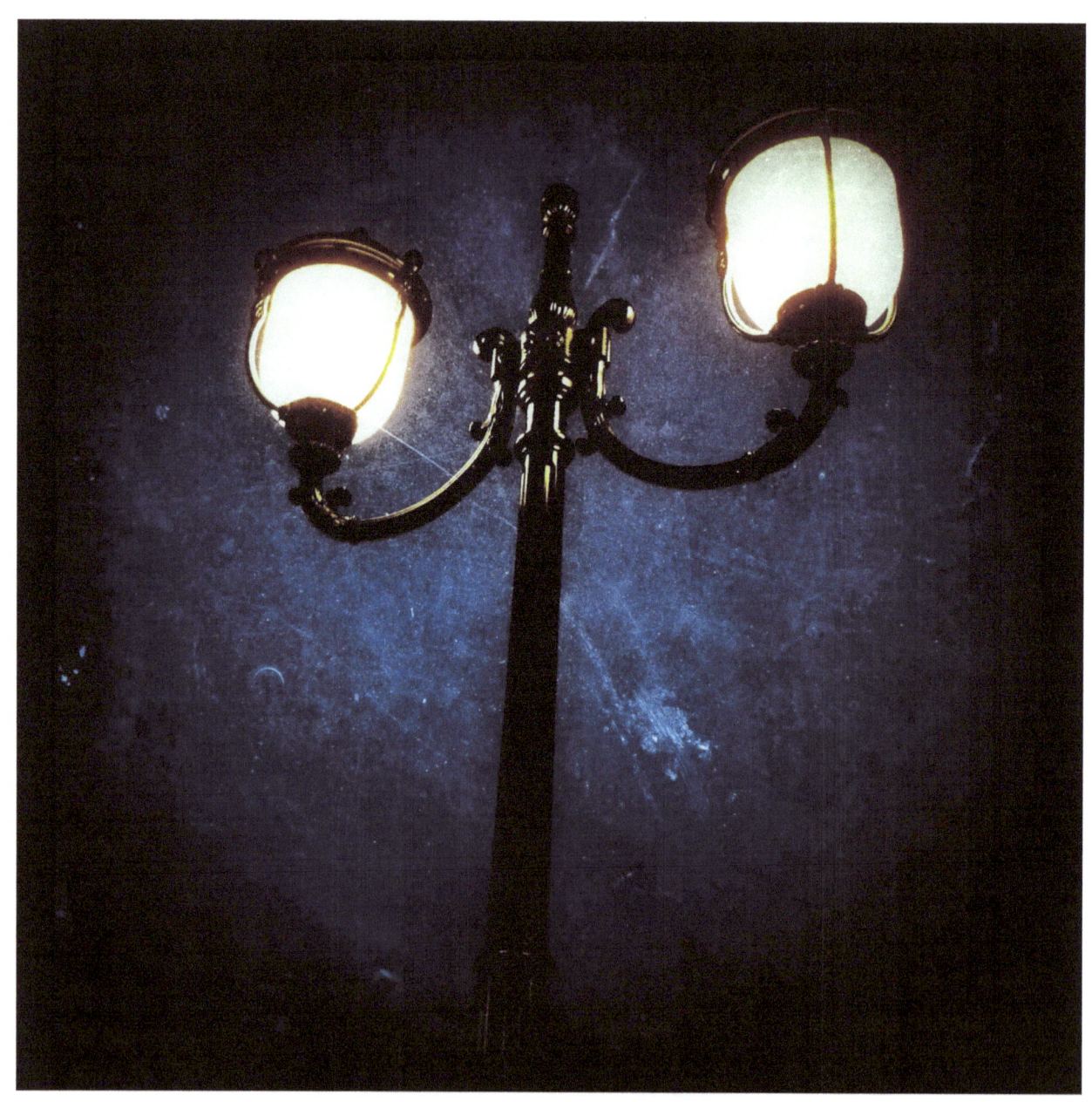

Crane's Roost

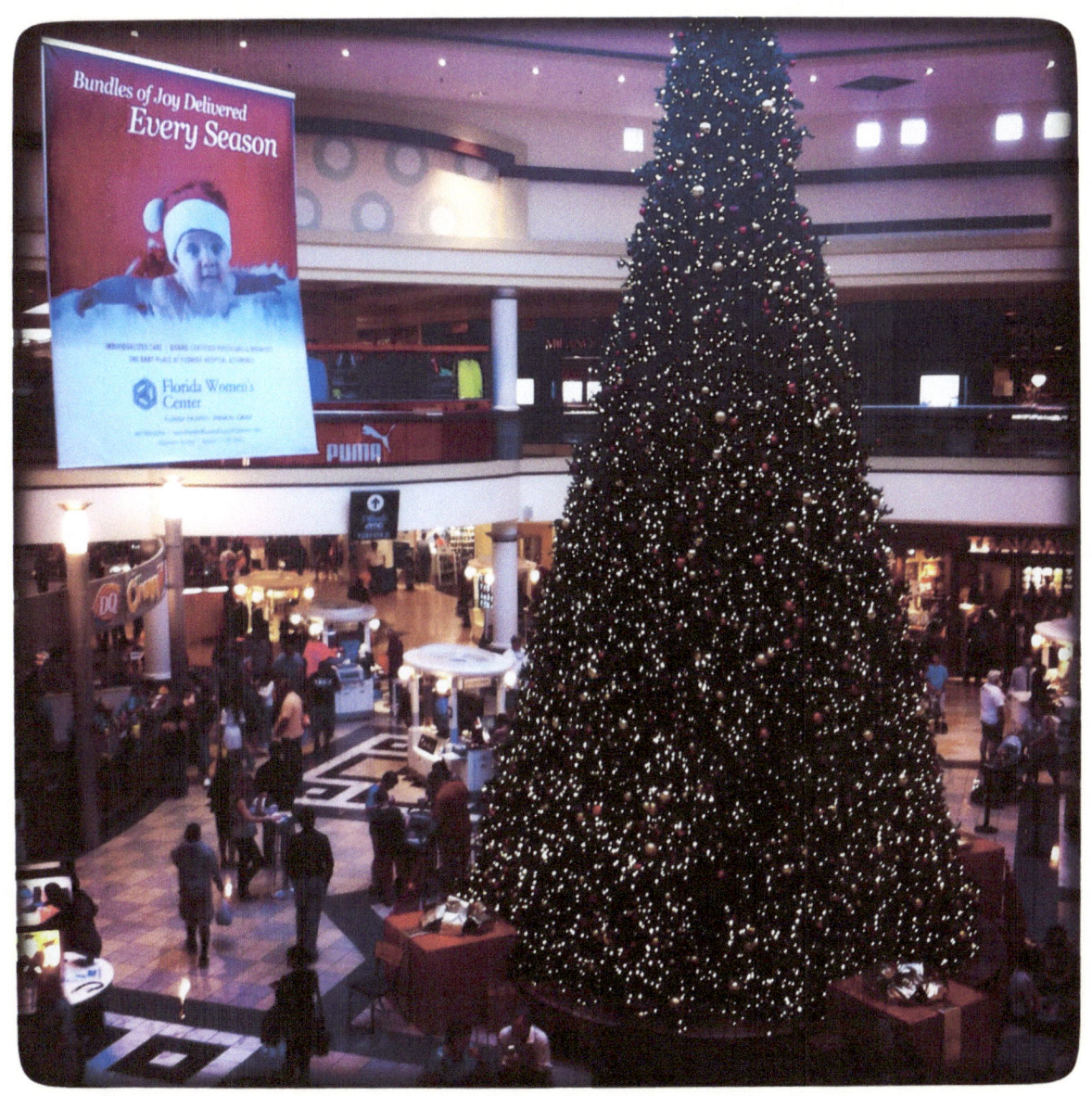

Altamonte Mall

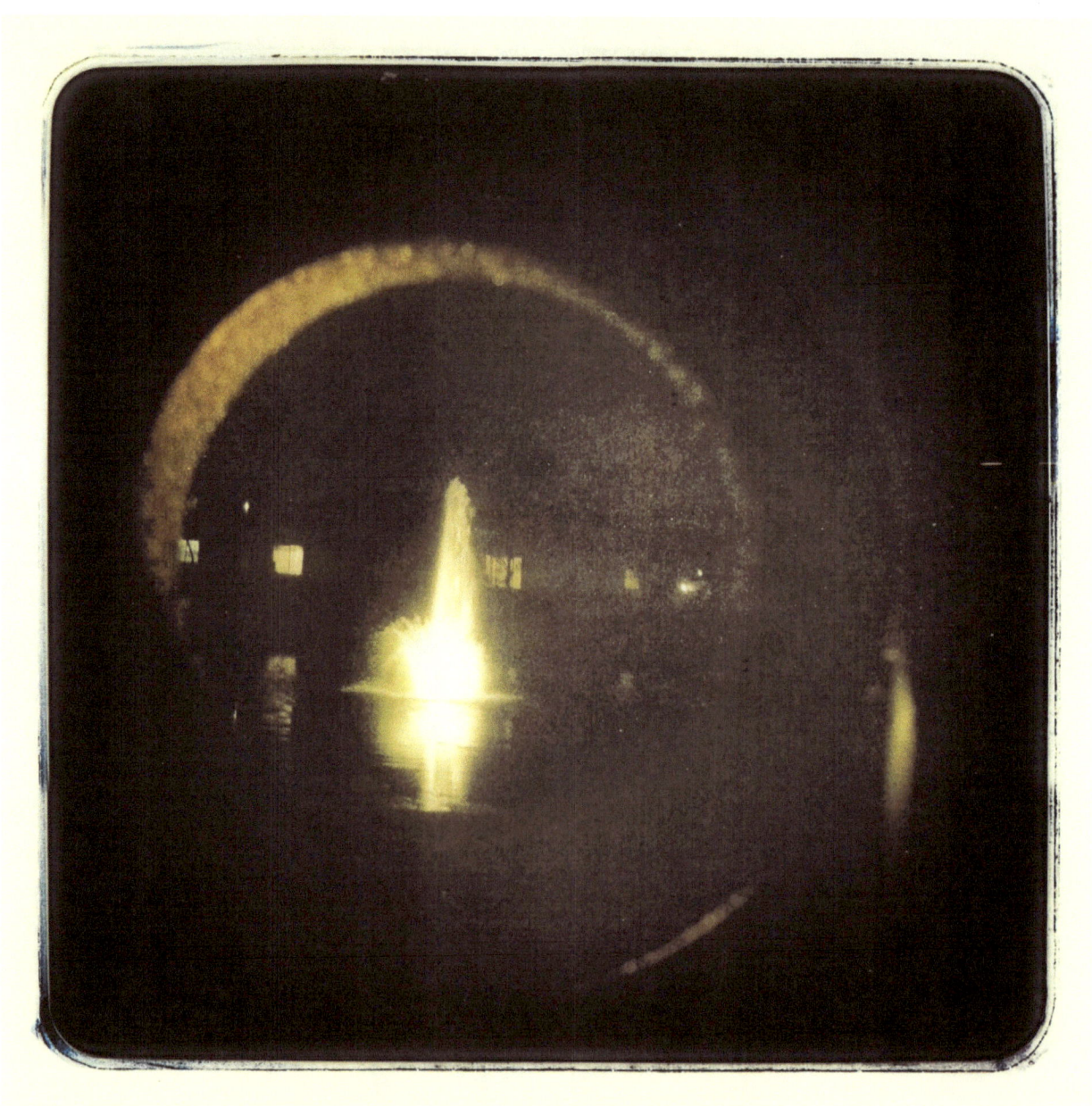

Fountain inside Camden Club

3.
Apopka, Florida

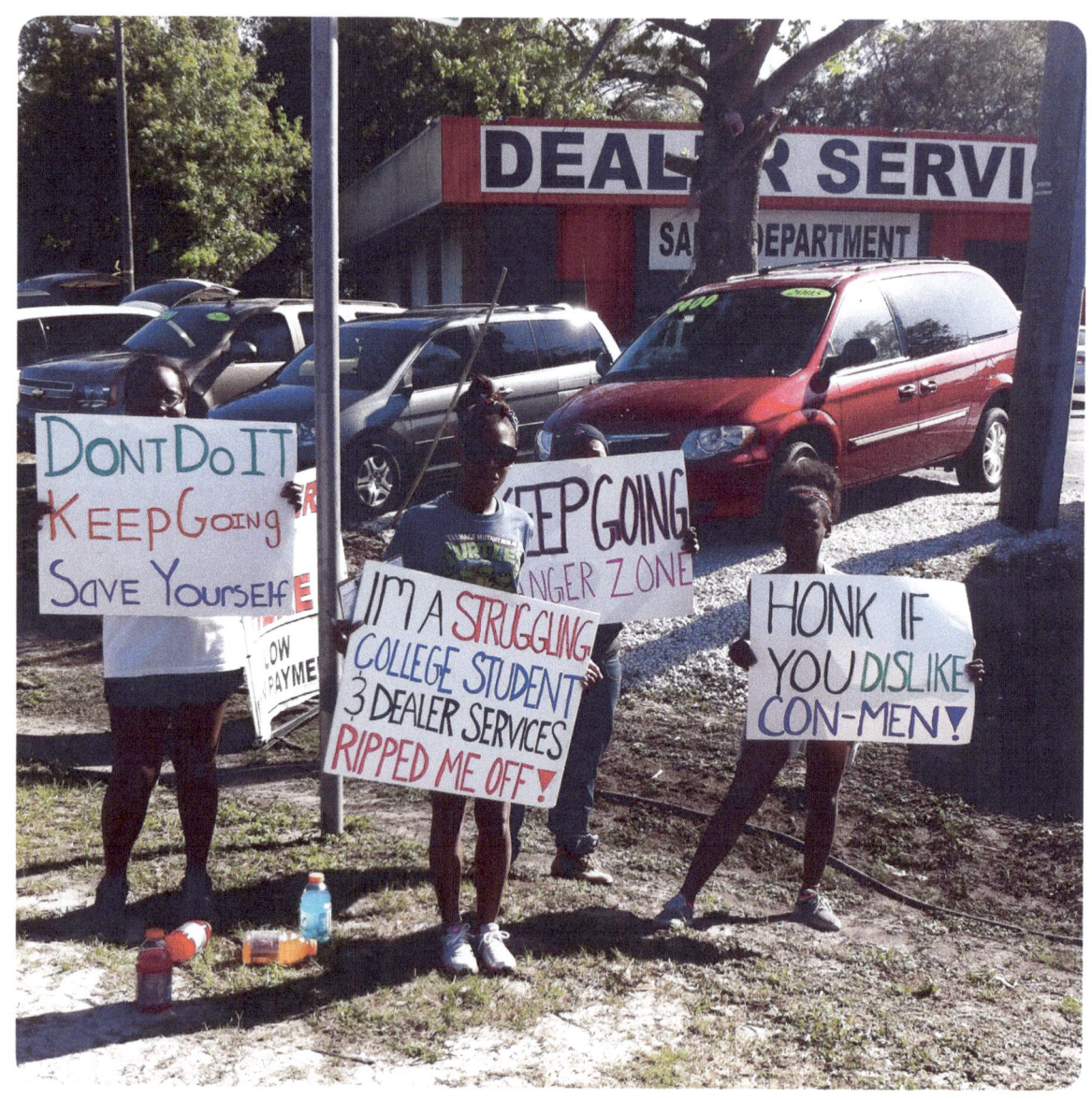

Picketing Dealer Services

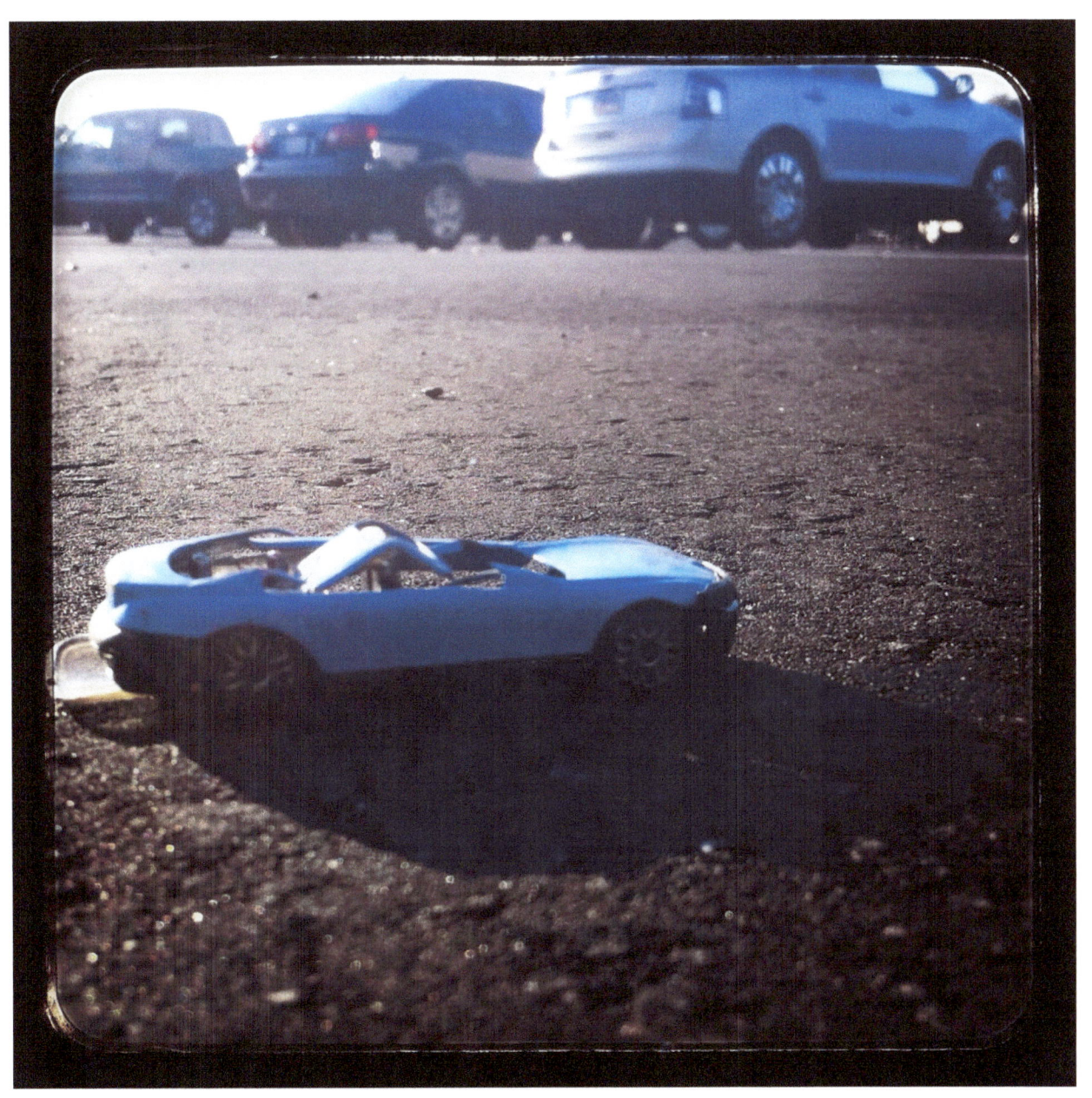

Super Wal-Mart Parking Lot

Super Wal-Mart Parking Lot

4.
Casselberry, Florida

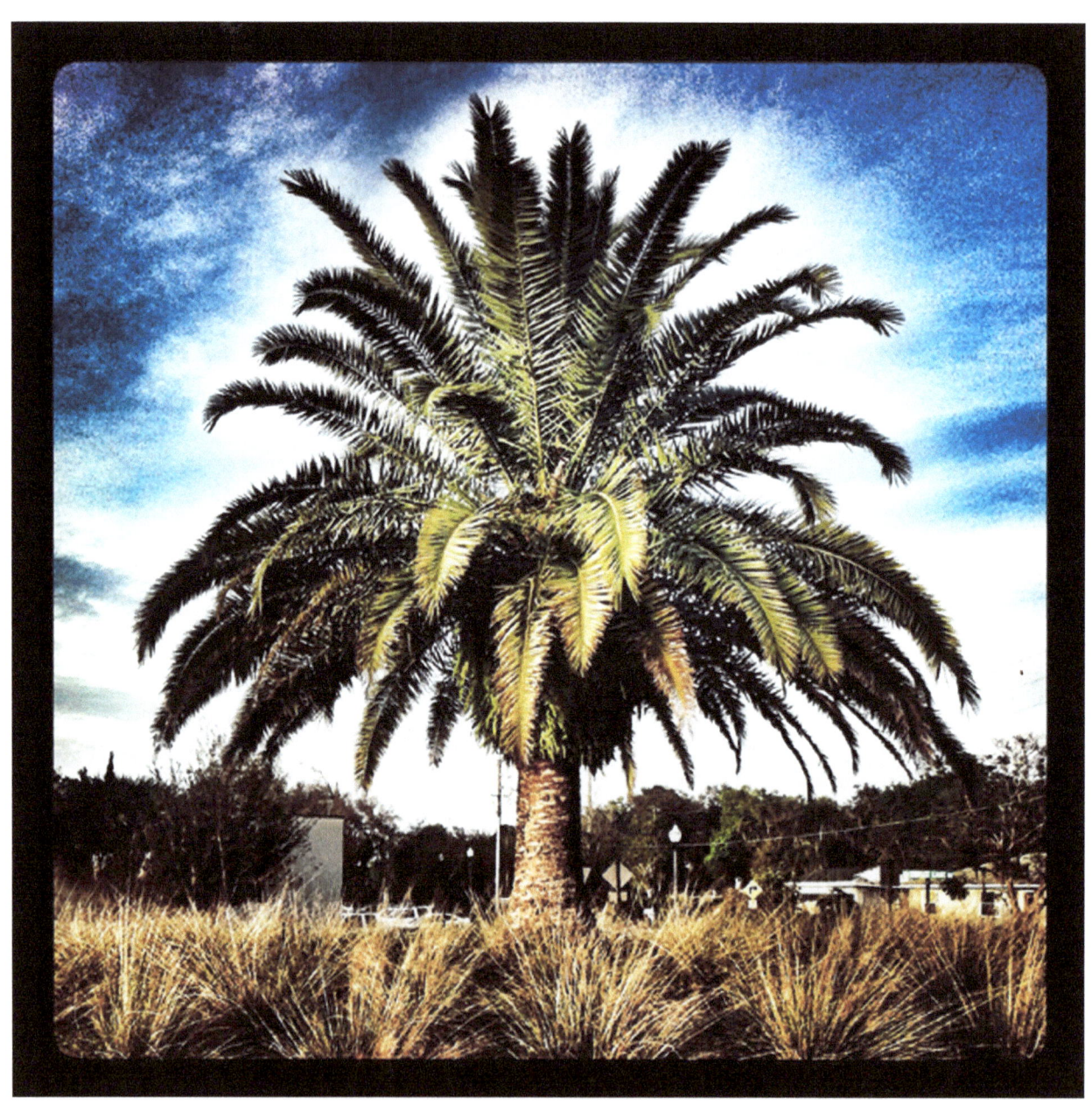

Canary Island Date Palm

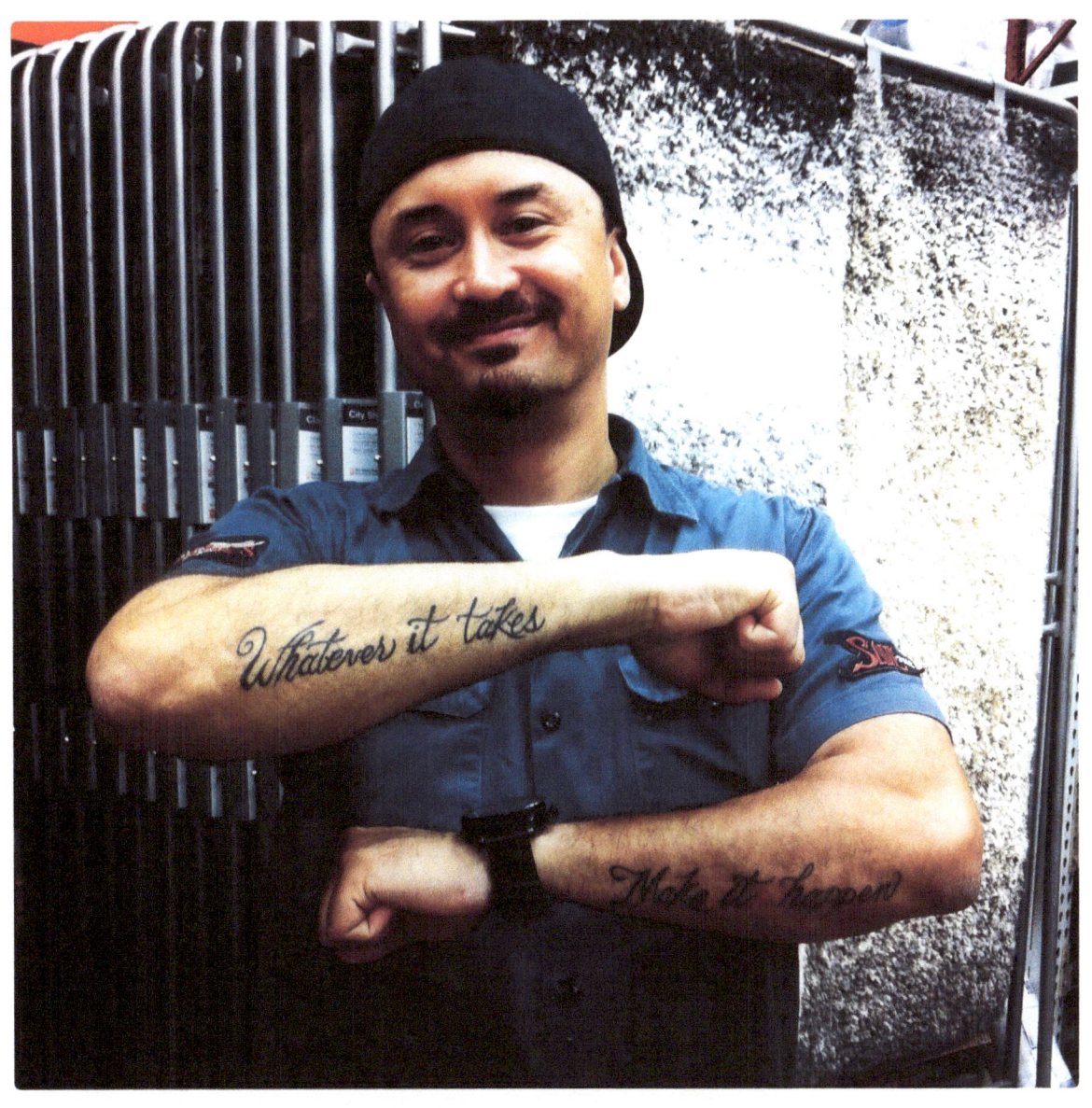

Jim Criger (Home Depot)

5.
Downtown Orlando, Florida

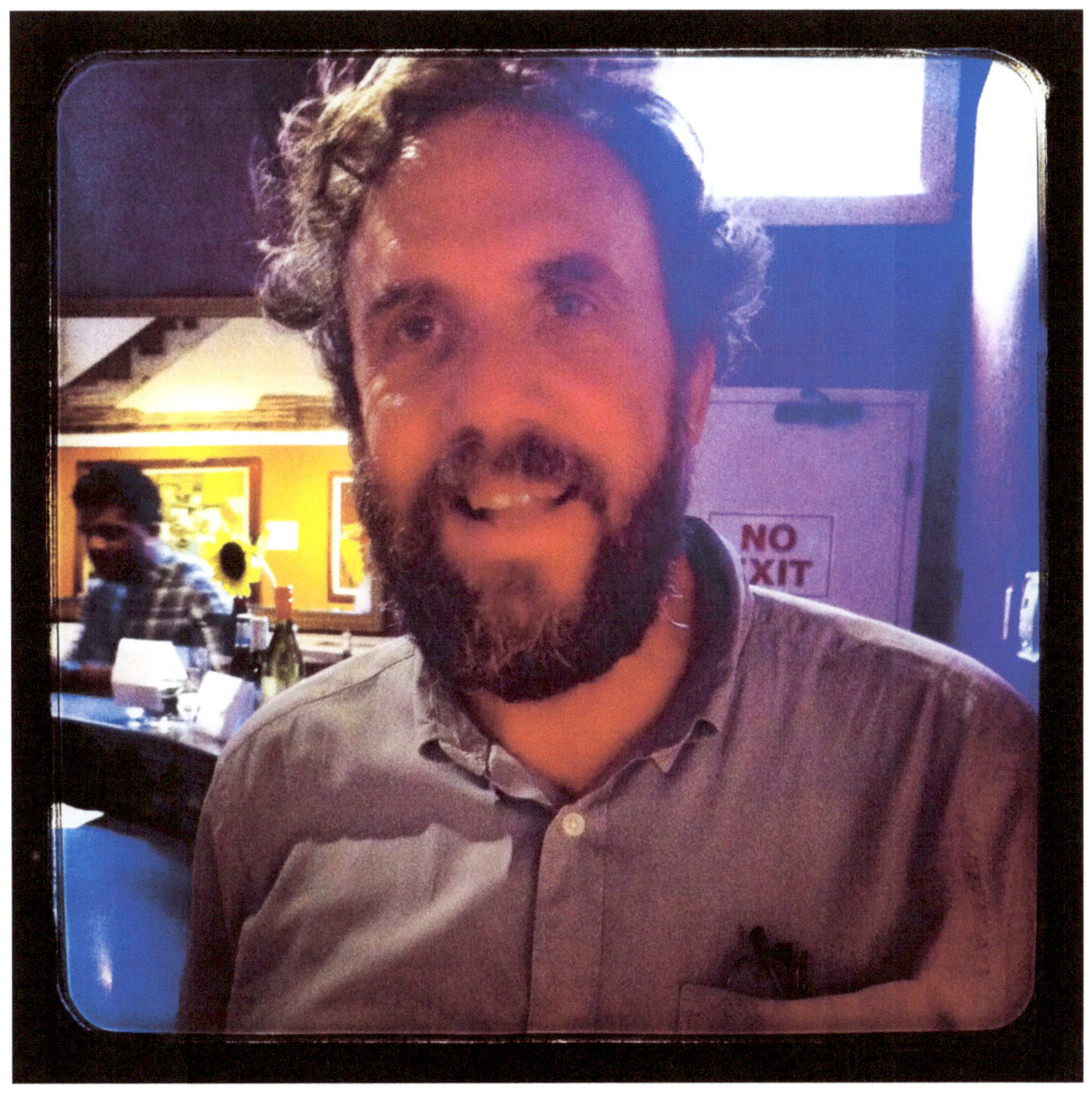

Gallery Director Patrick Greene
(The Gallery at Avalon Island)

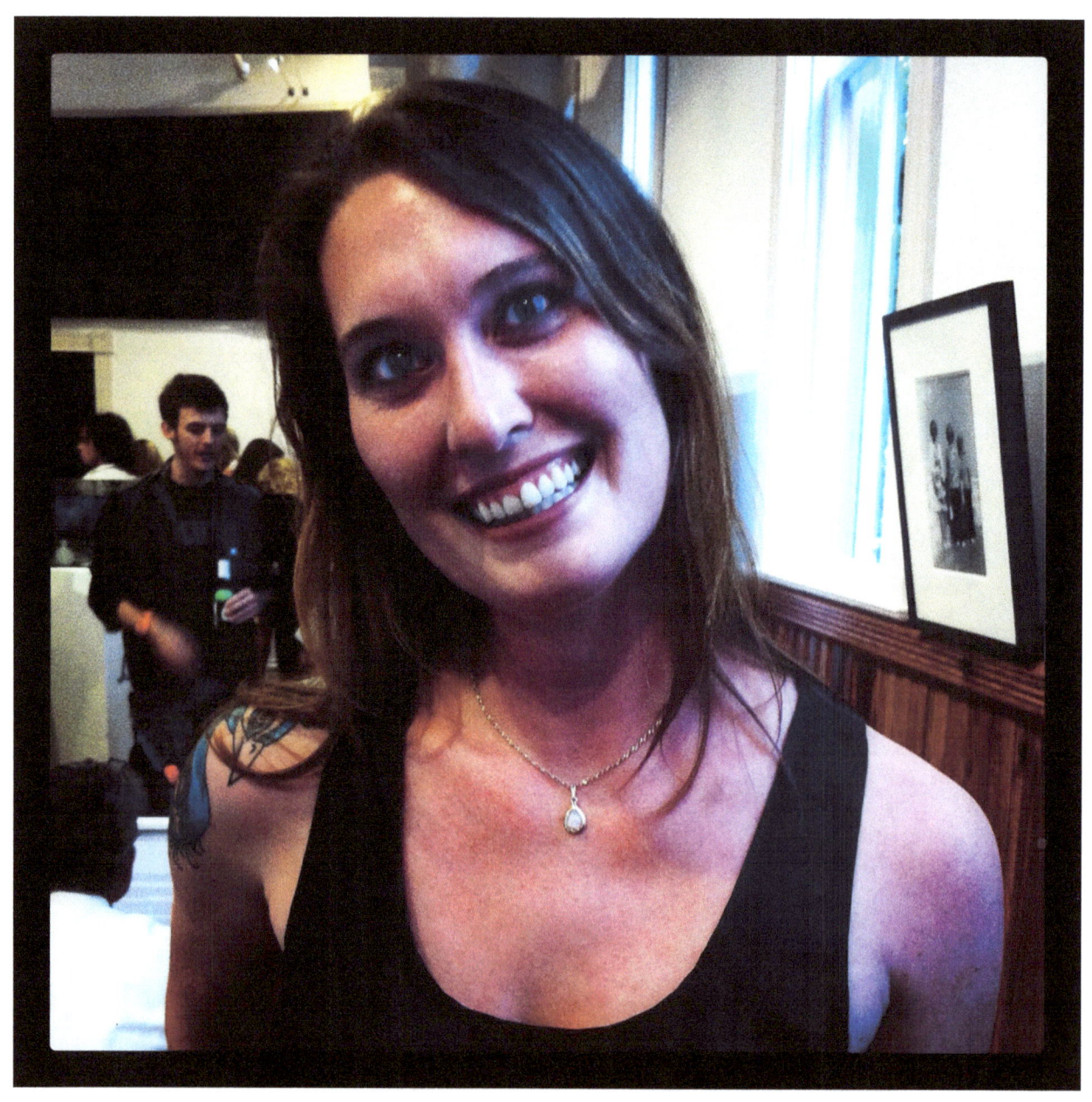

Artist Kayla Prommersberger
(The Gallery at Avalon Island)

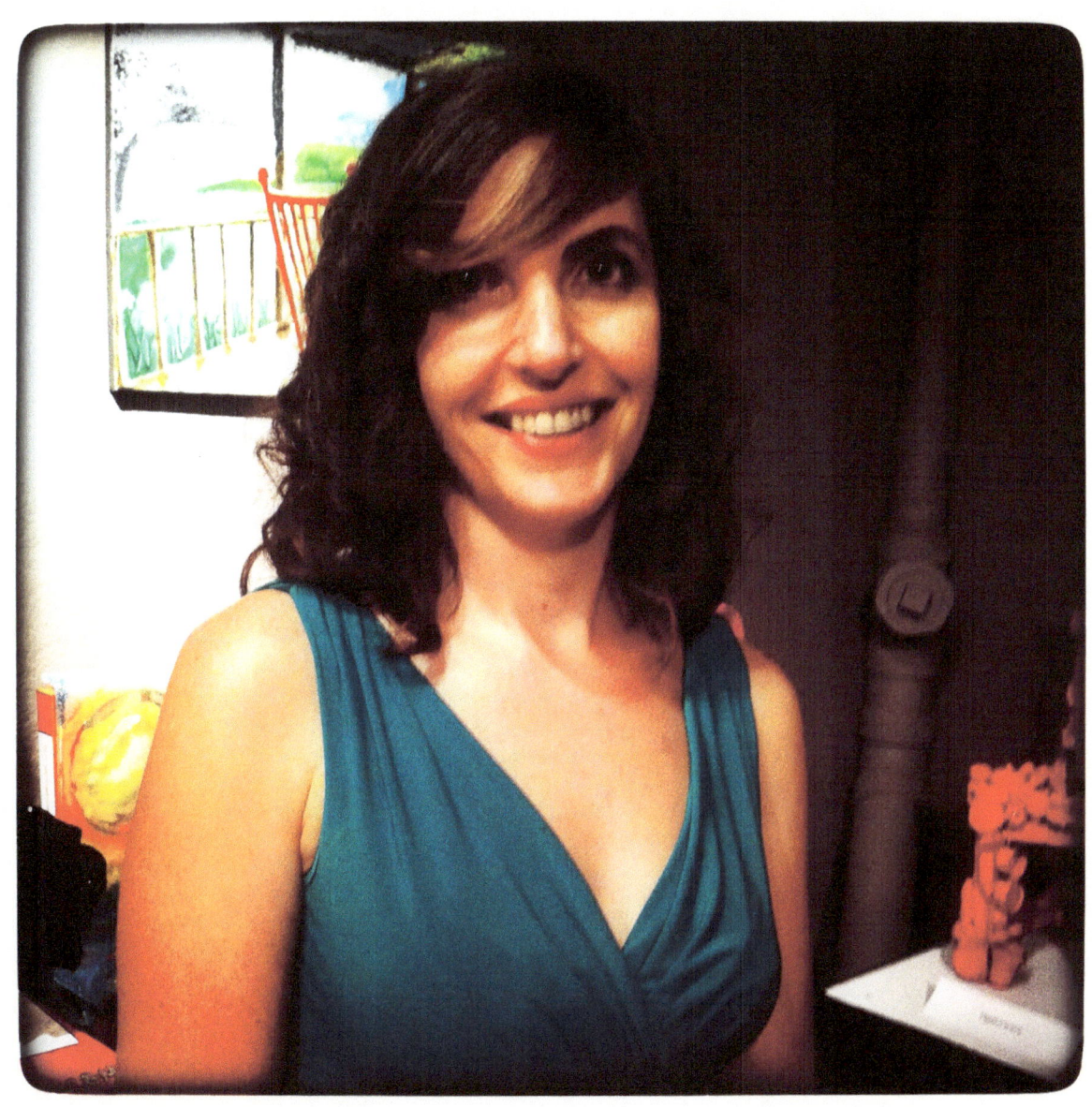

Artist Heather Ashworth Pereira
(City Arts Factory)

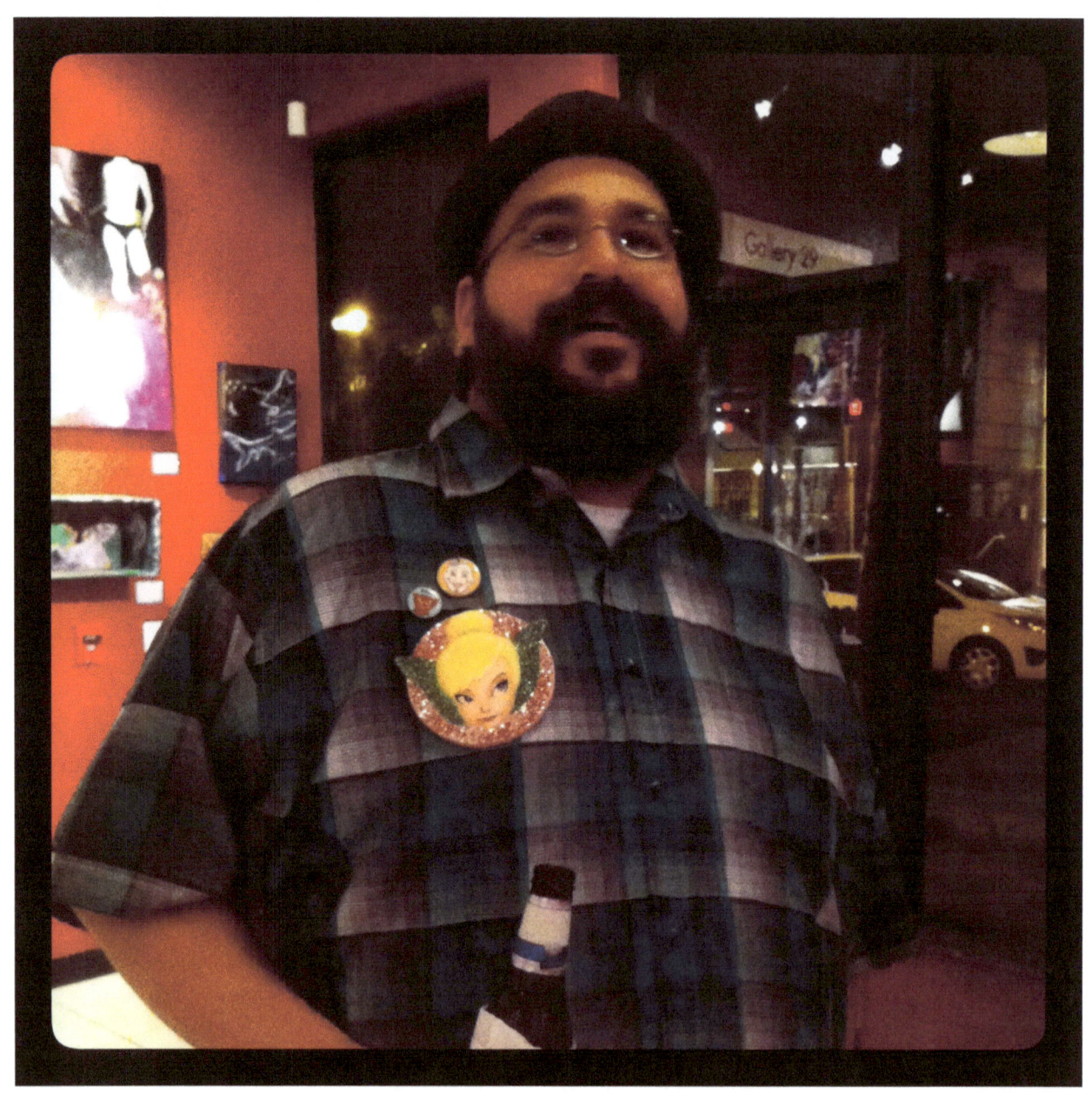

Artist Cake Marques (City Arts Factory)

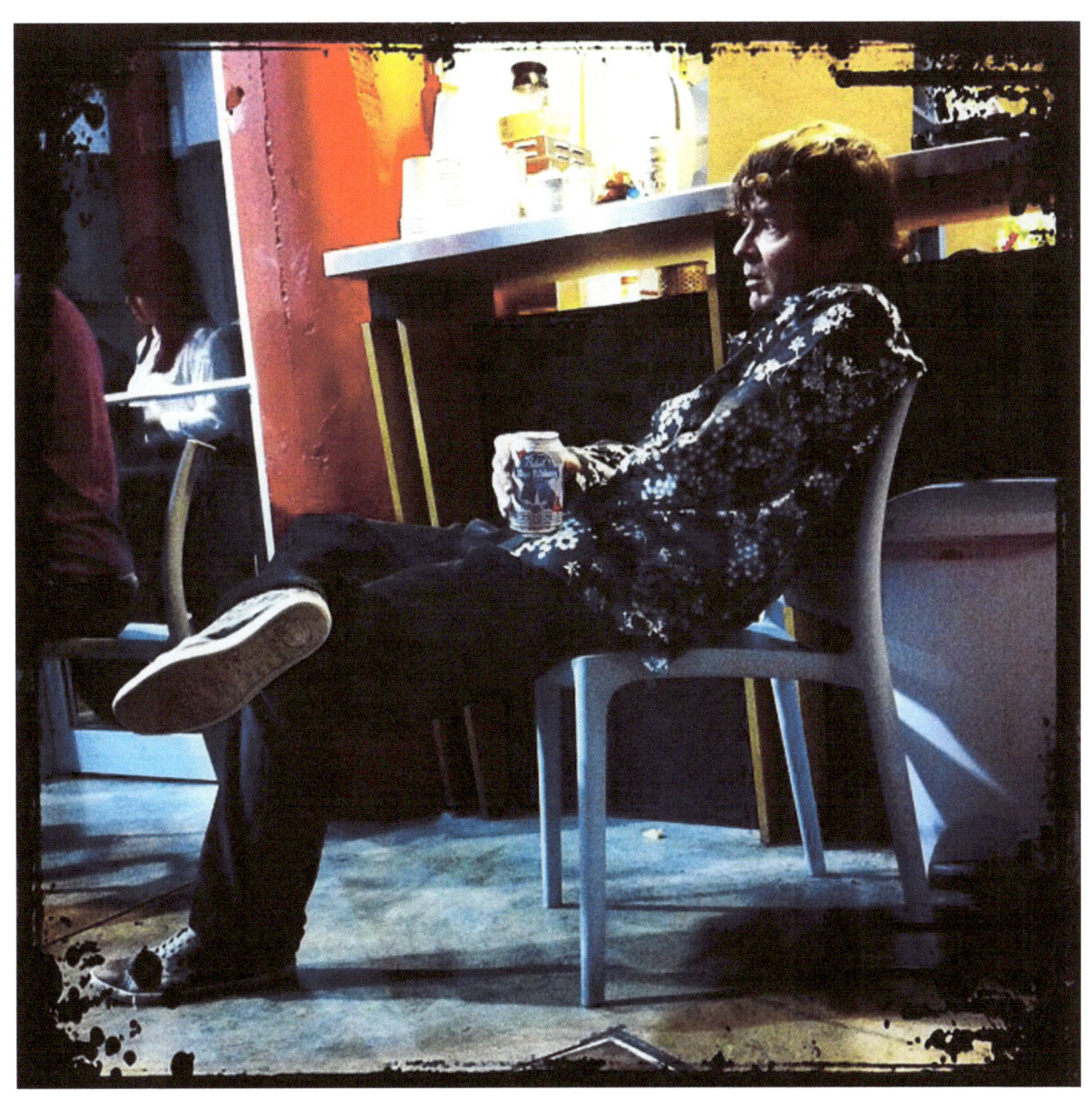

Artist Morgan Steele (Urban Rethink)

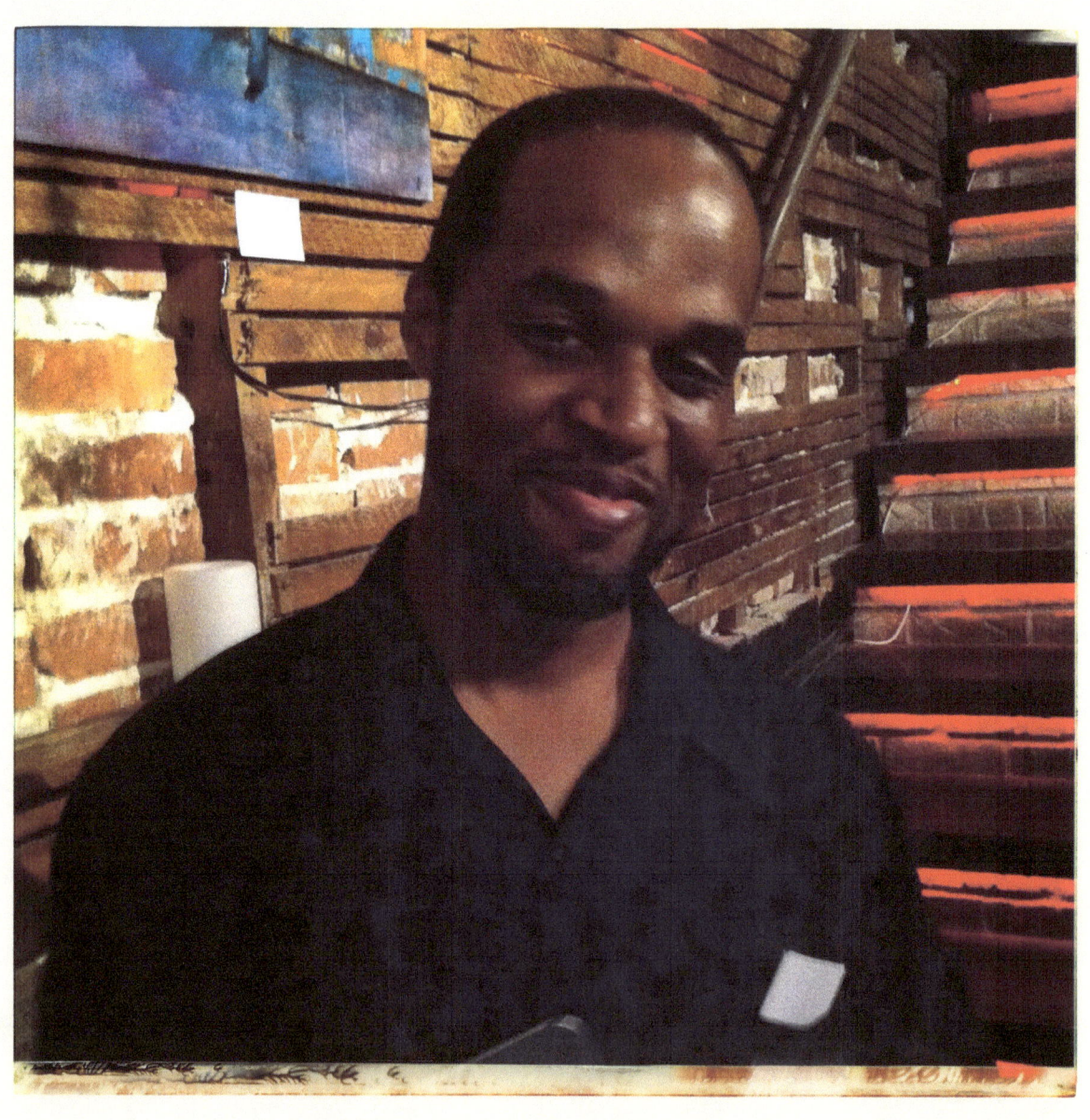

Artist/Curator TrezMark Harris (NV Art Bar)

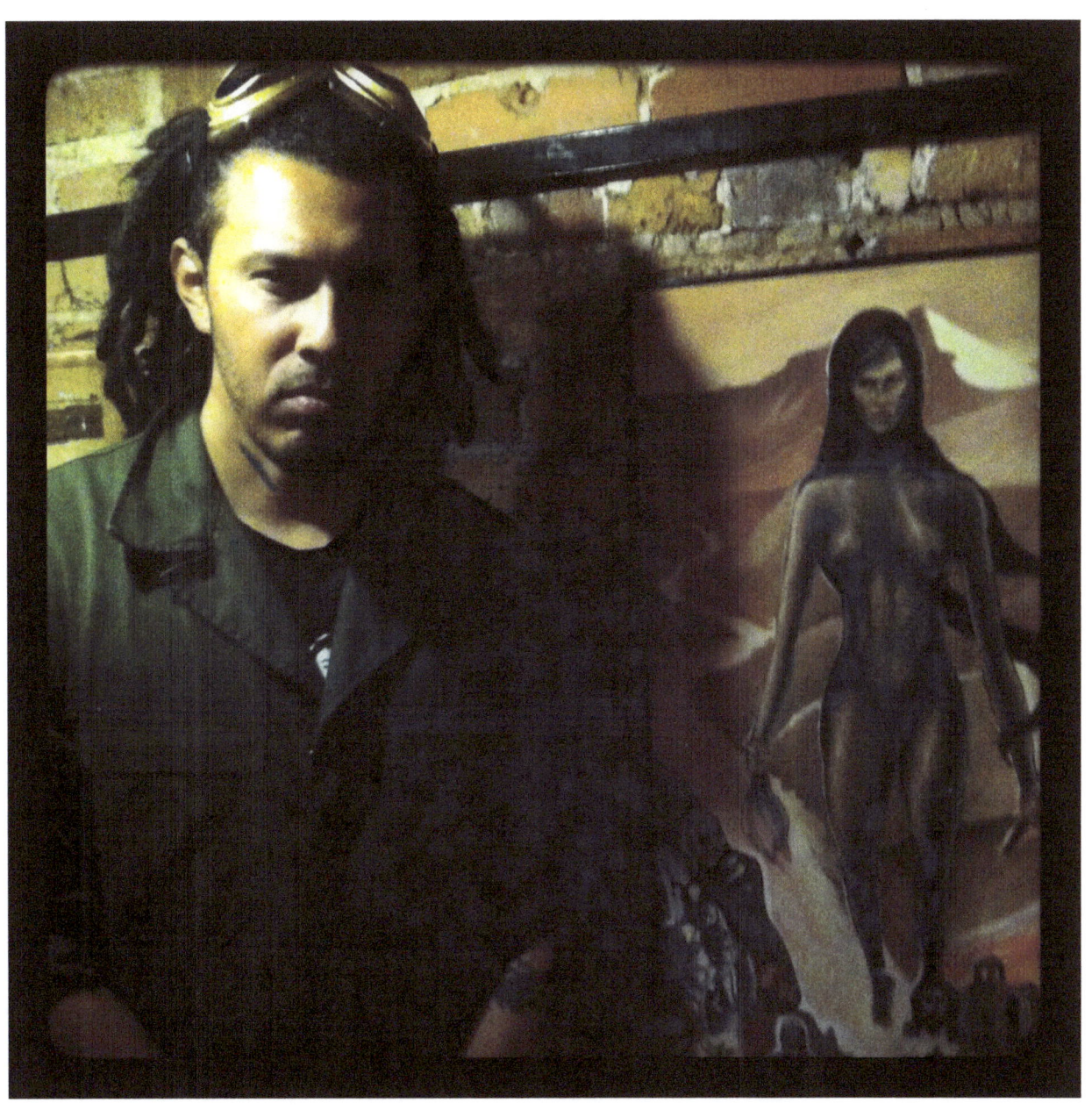

Artist German Lemus (NV Art Bar)

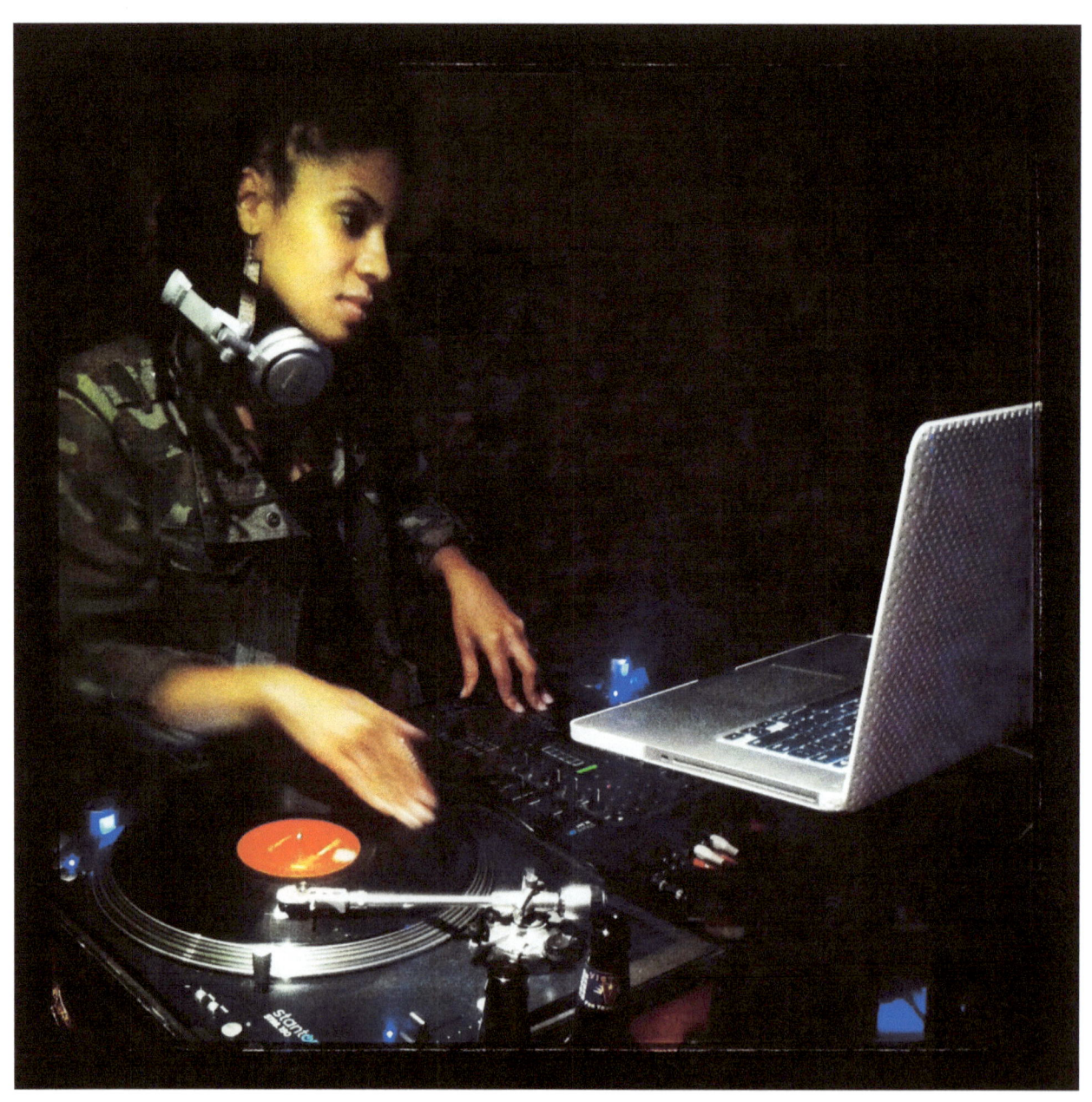

Eve (NV Art Bar)

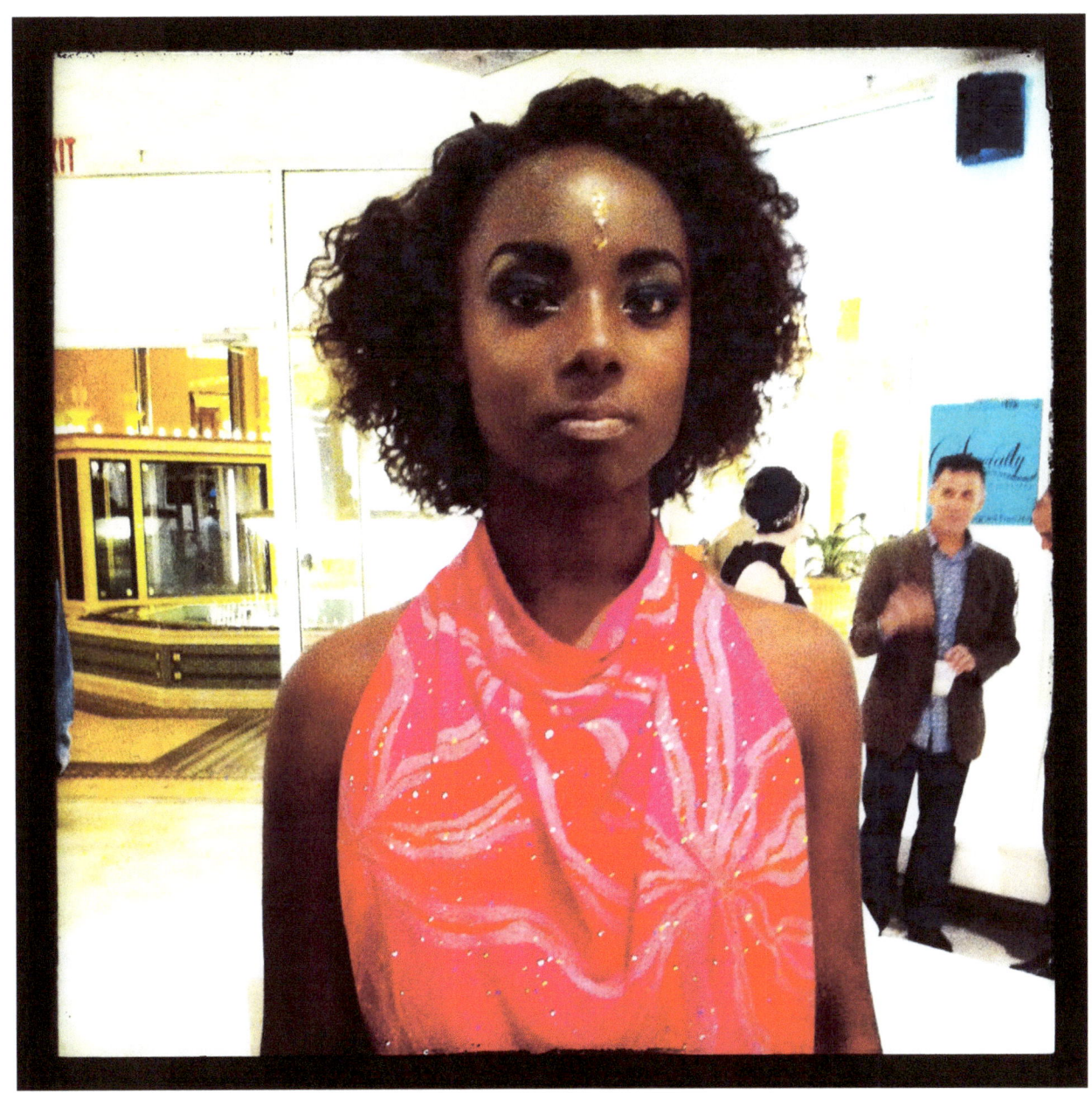

Fashion Model (Jai Gallery)

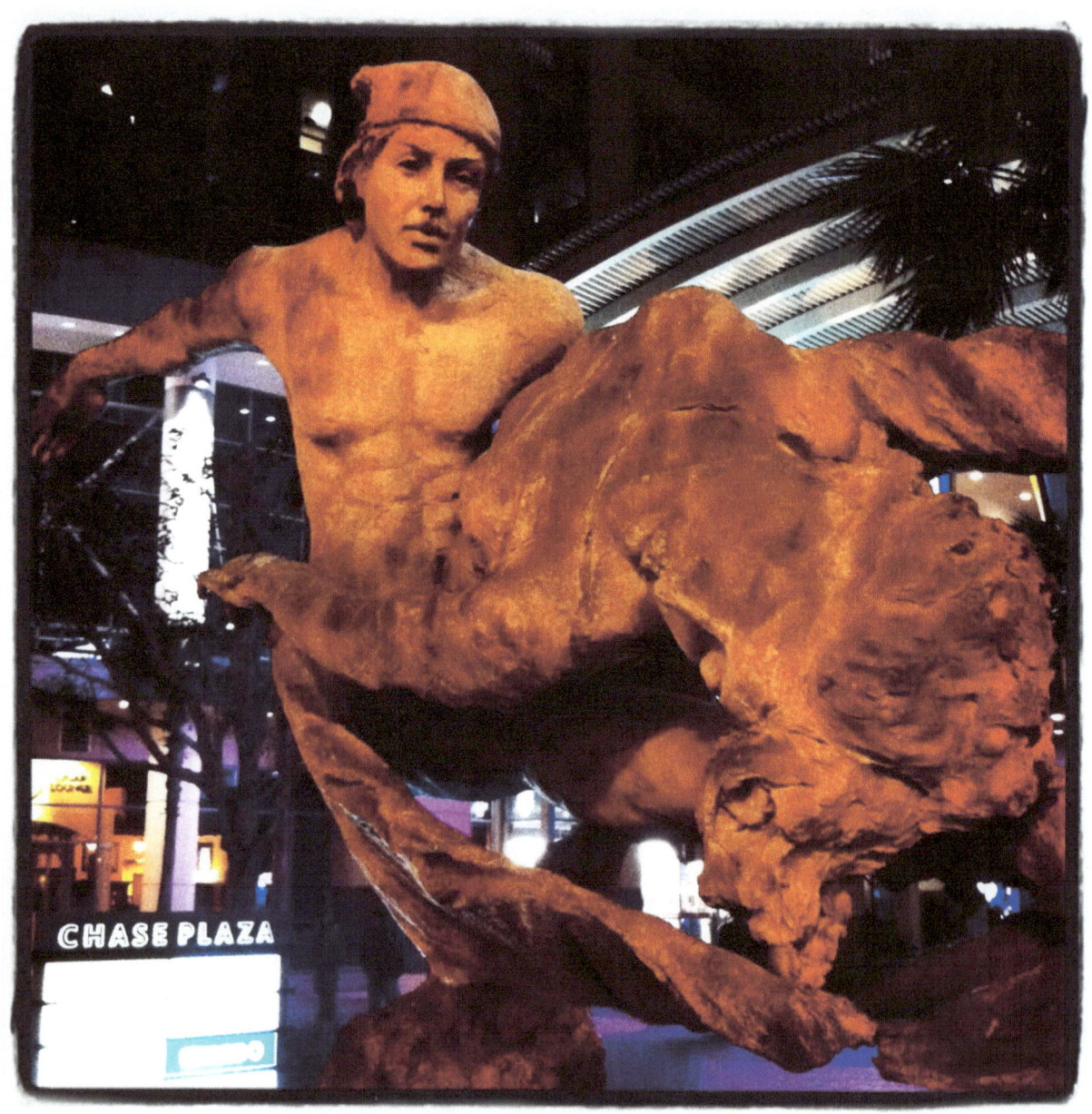

Chase Plaza

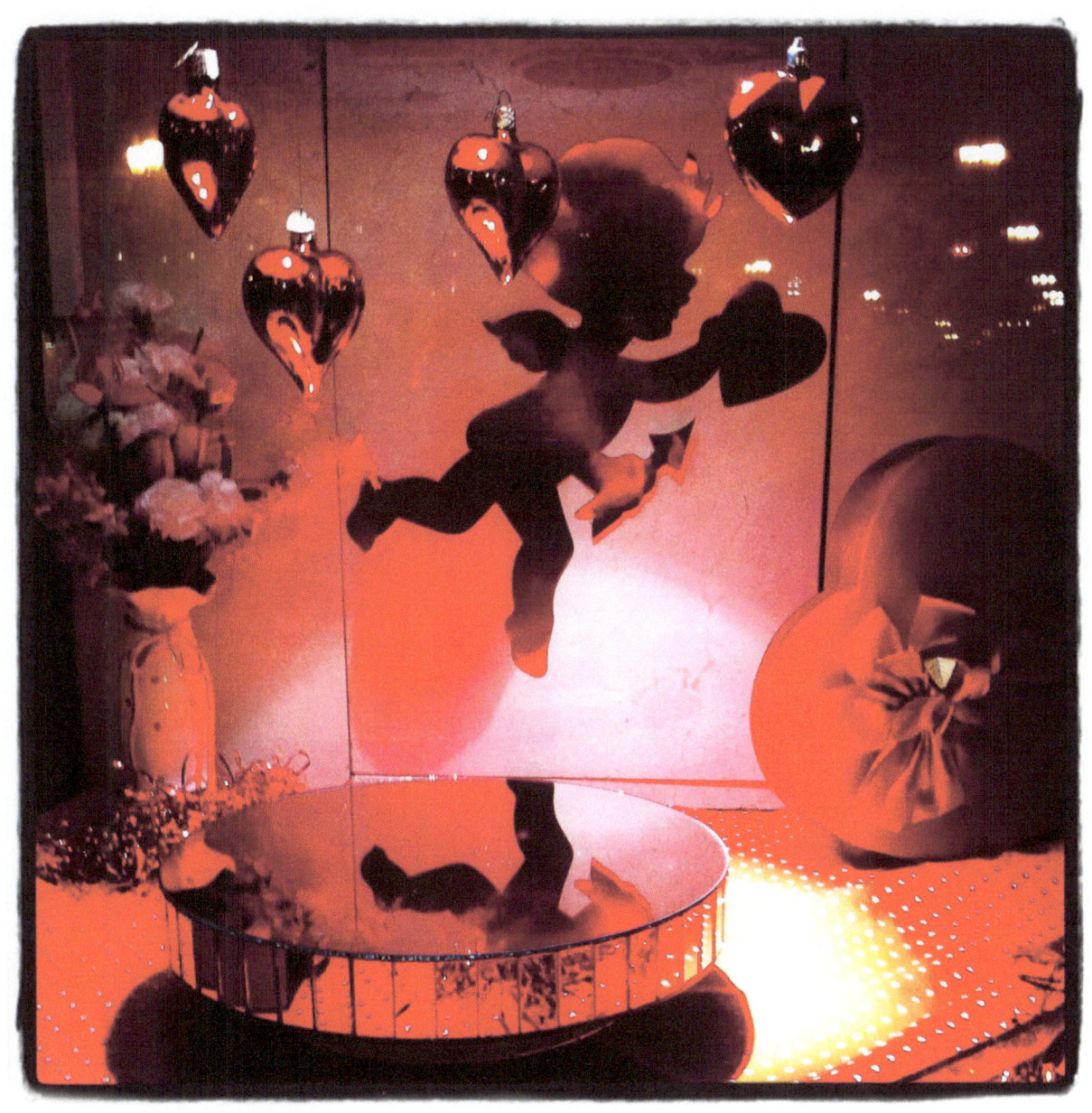

Window Display (Swalstead, I think)

Orange Avenue

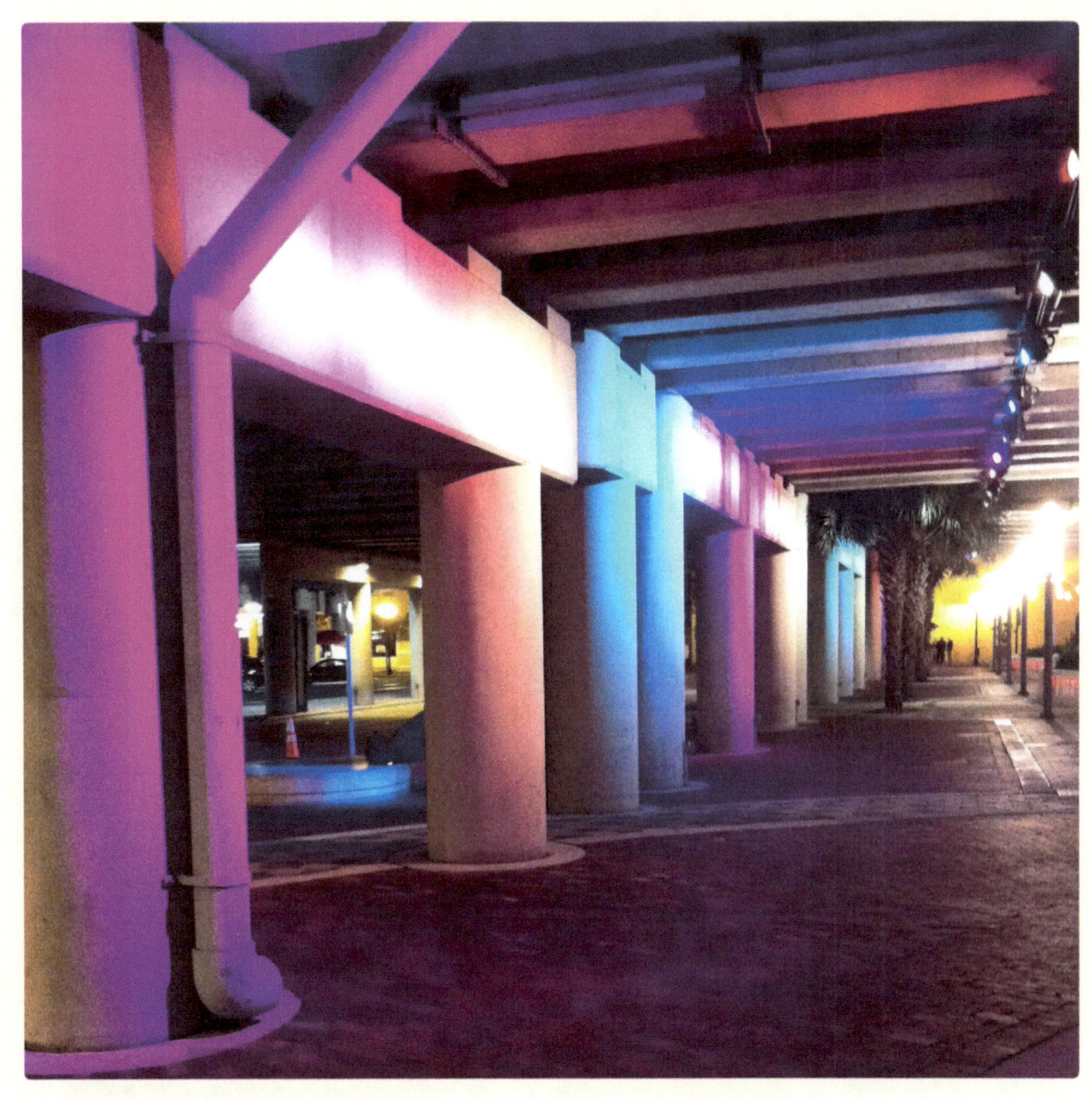

Underneath Interstate 4

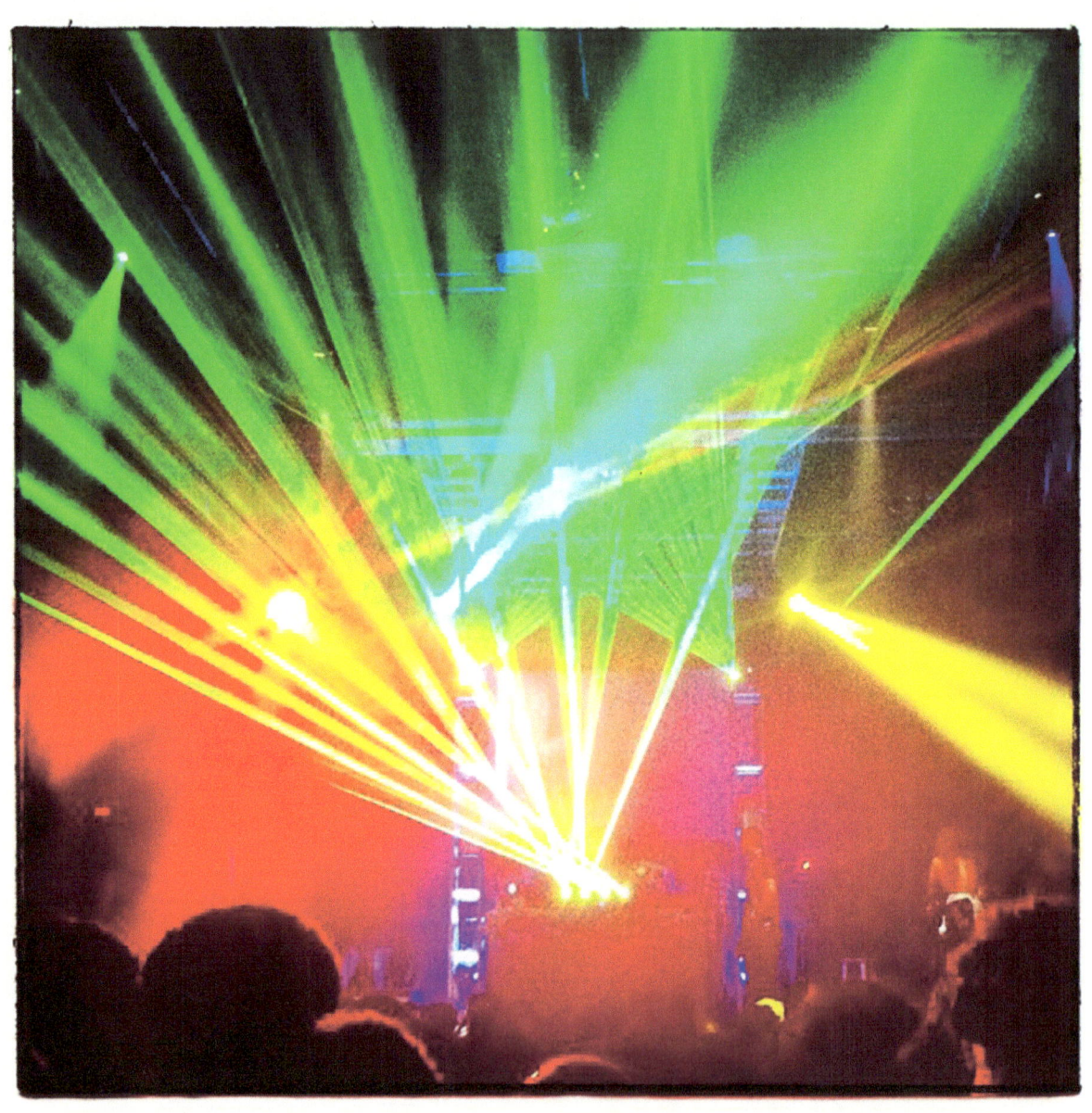

The Beacham

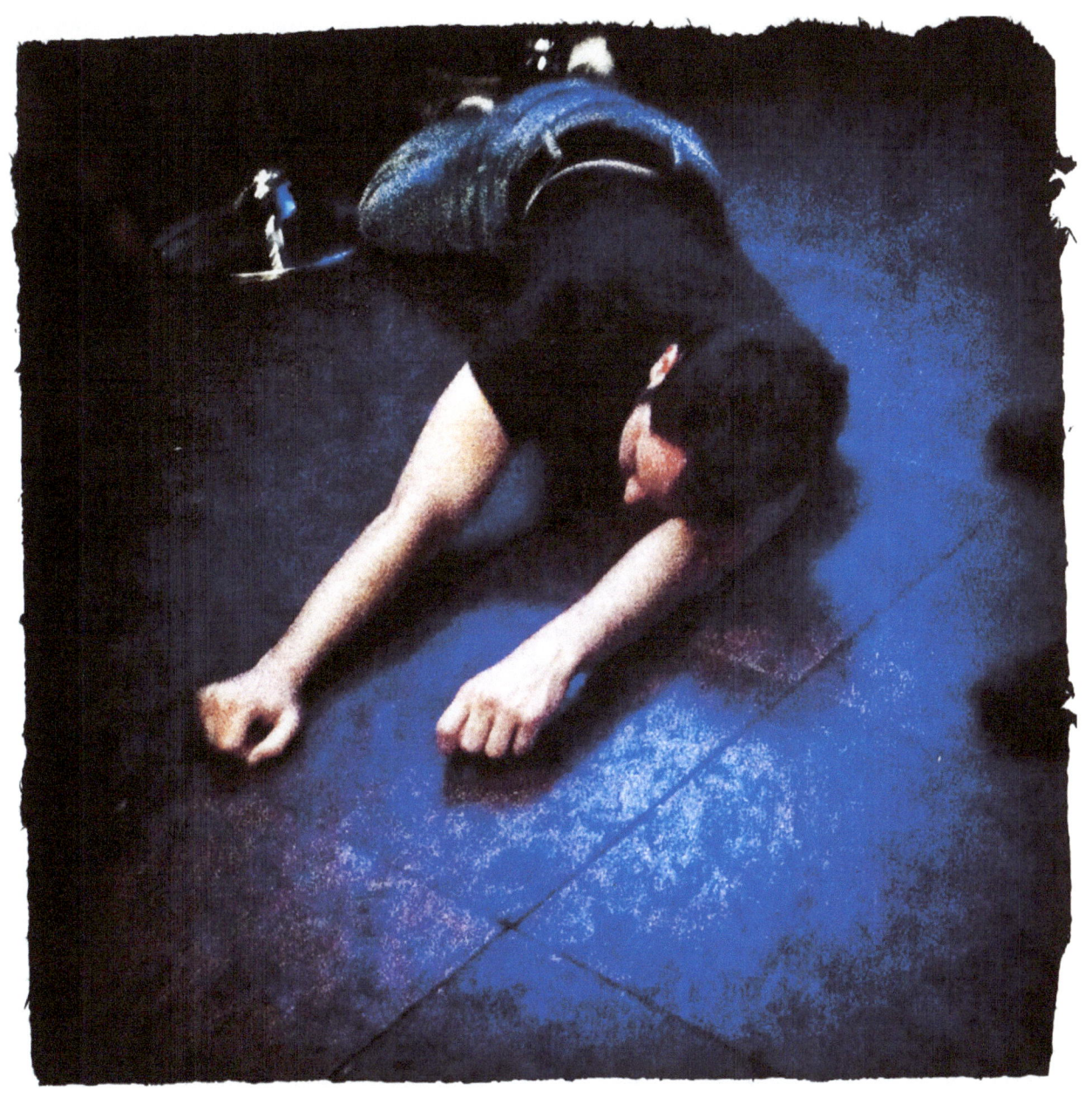

Knocked Out (Beth's Burger Bar)

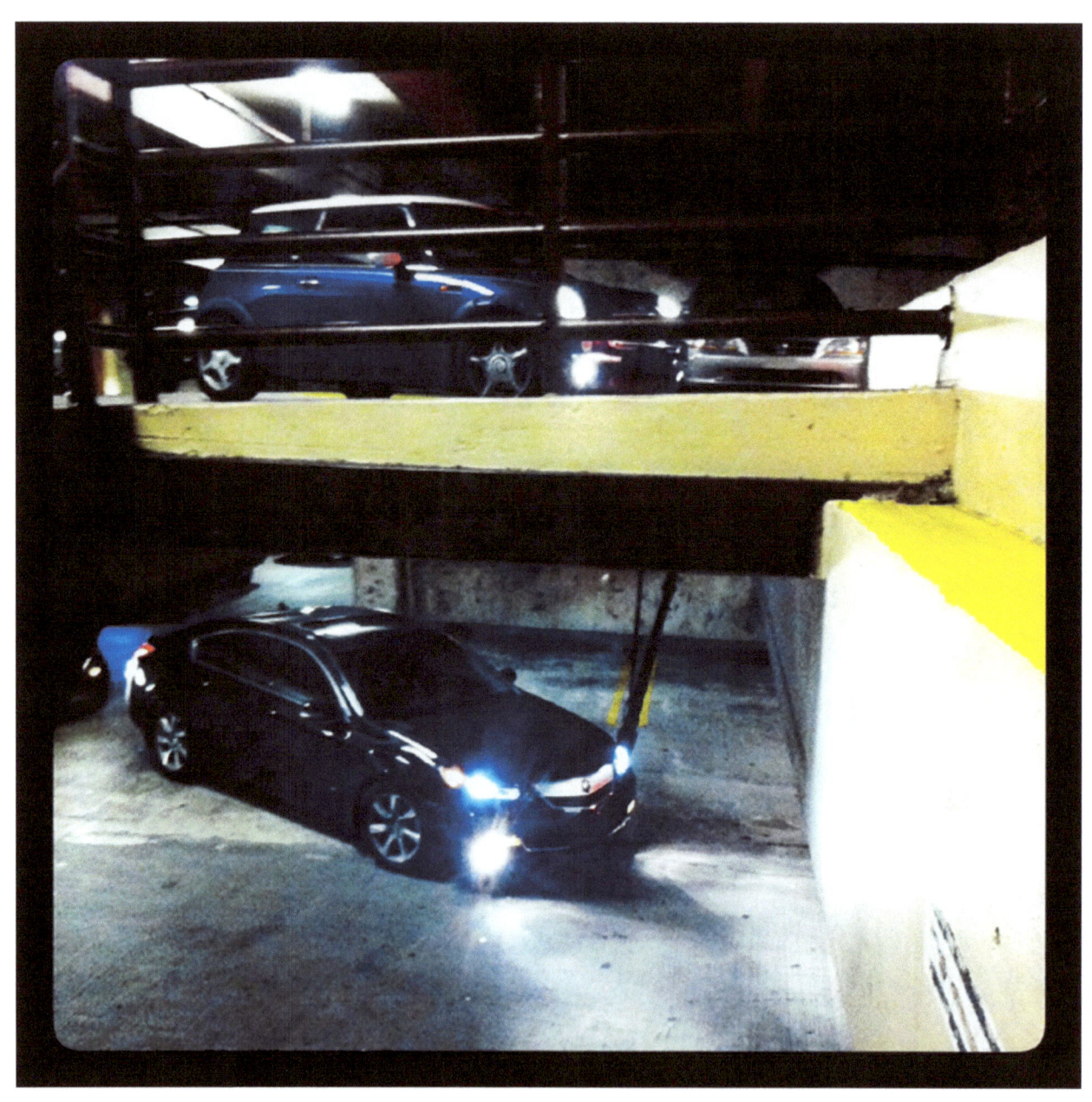

Parking Garage. Heading Home.

6.
Mills Avenue, Orlando, Florida

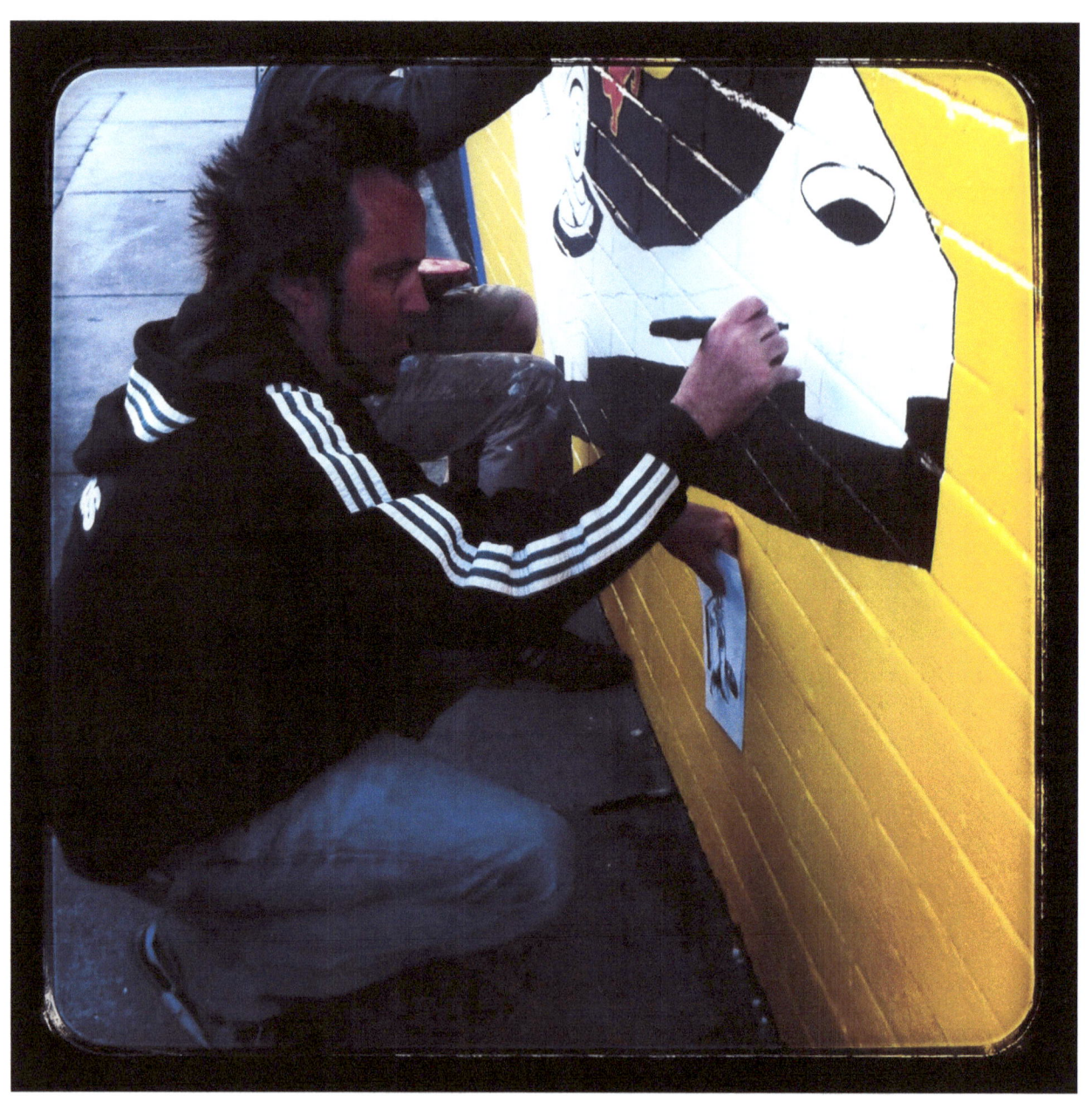

Muralist and Illustrator Andrew Spear

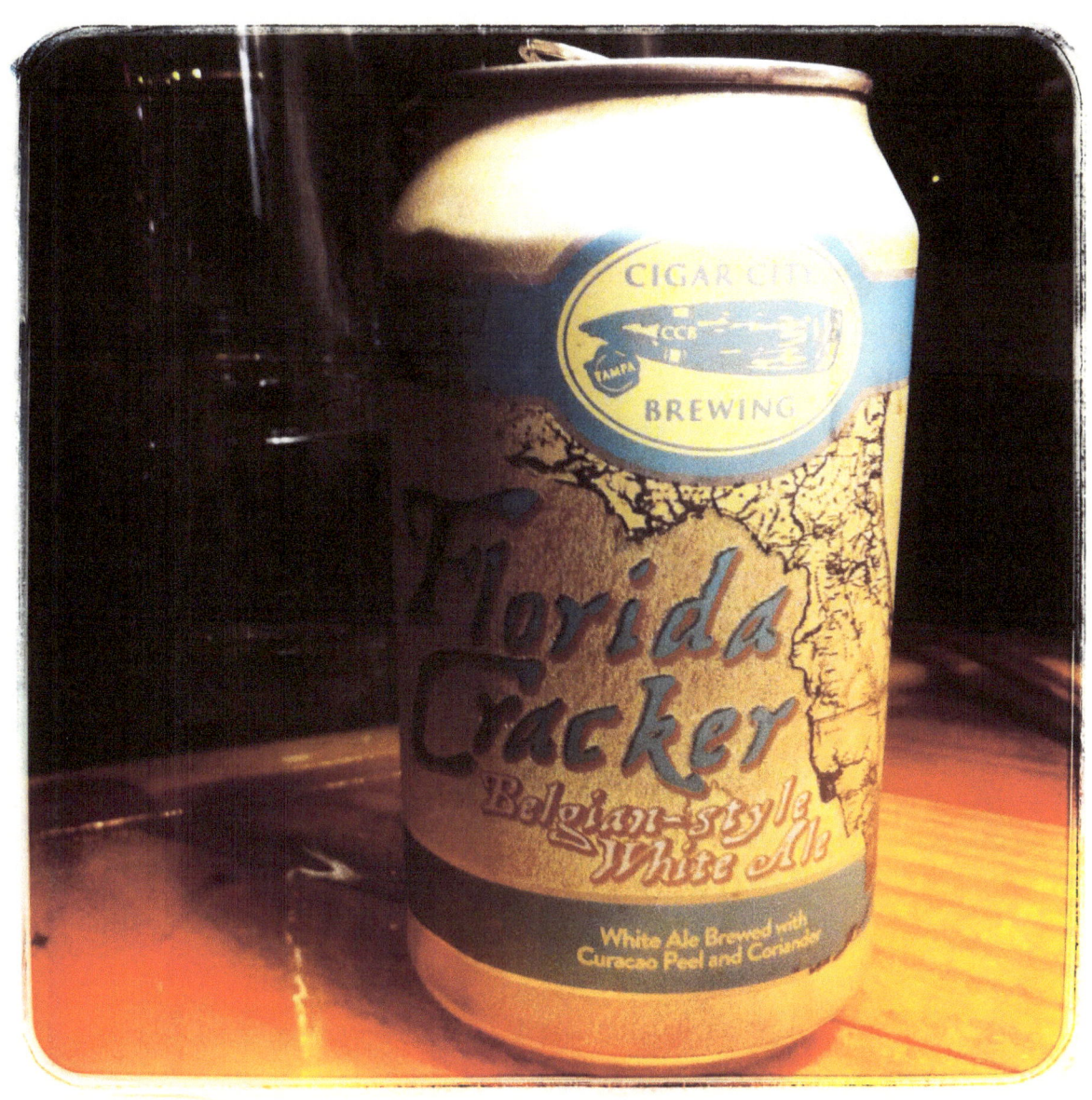

Drunk one myself. (Lil Indies)

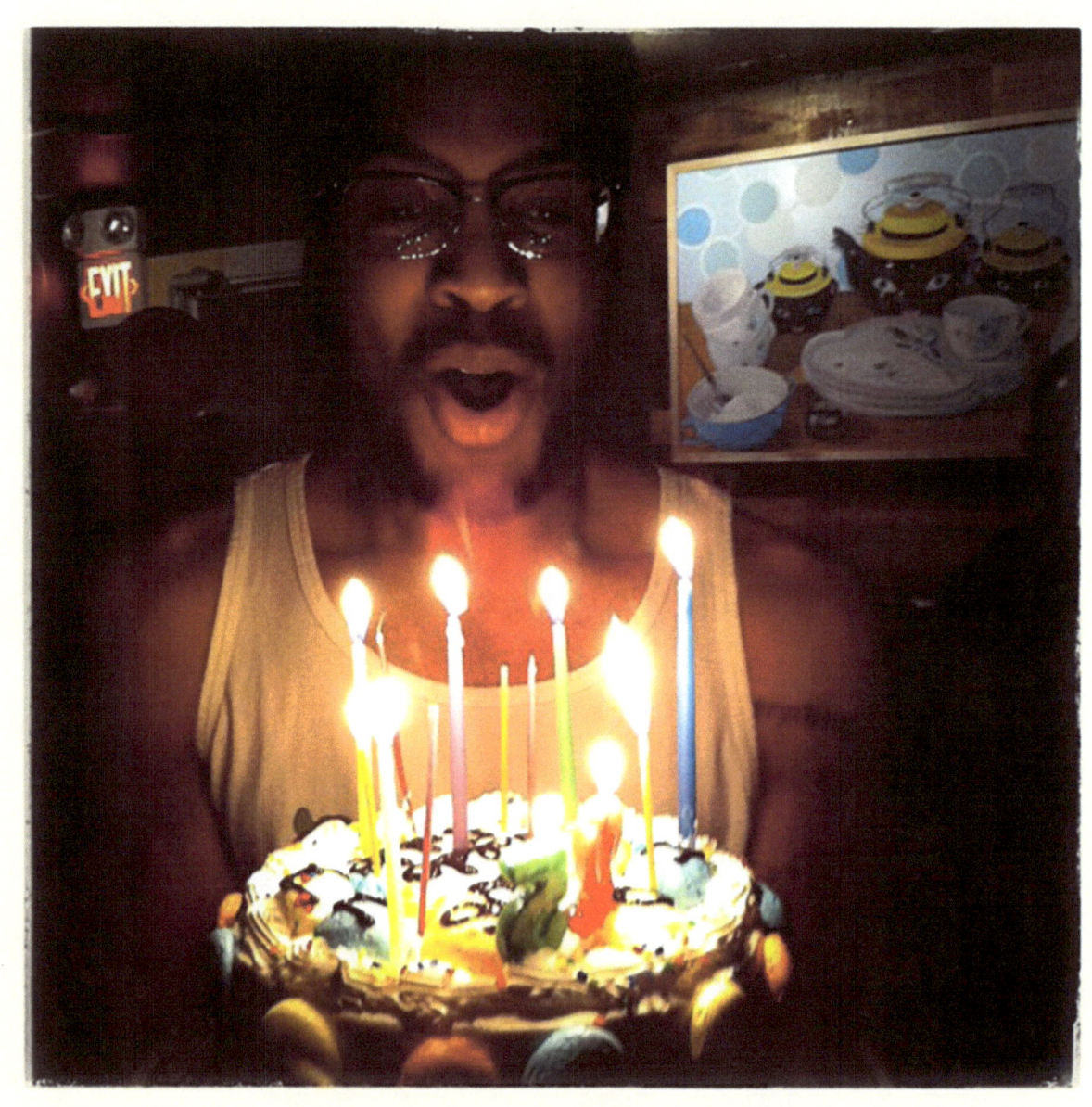

DJ Waldo Faldo (Lil Indies)

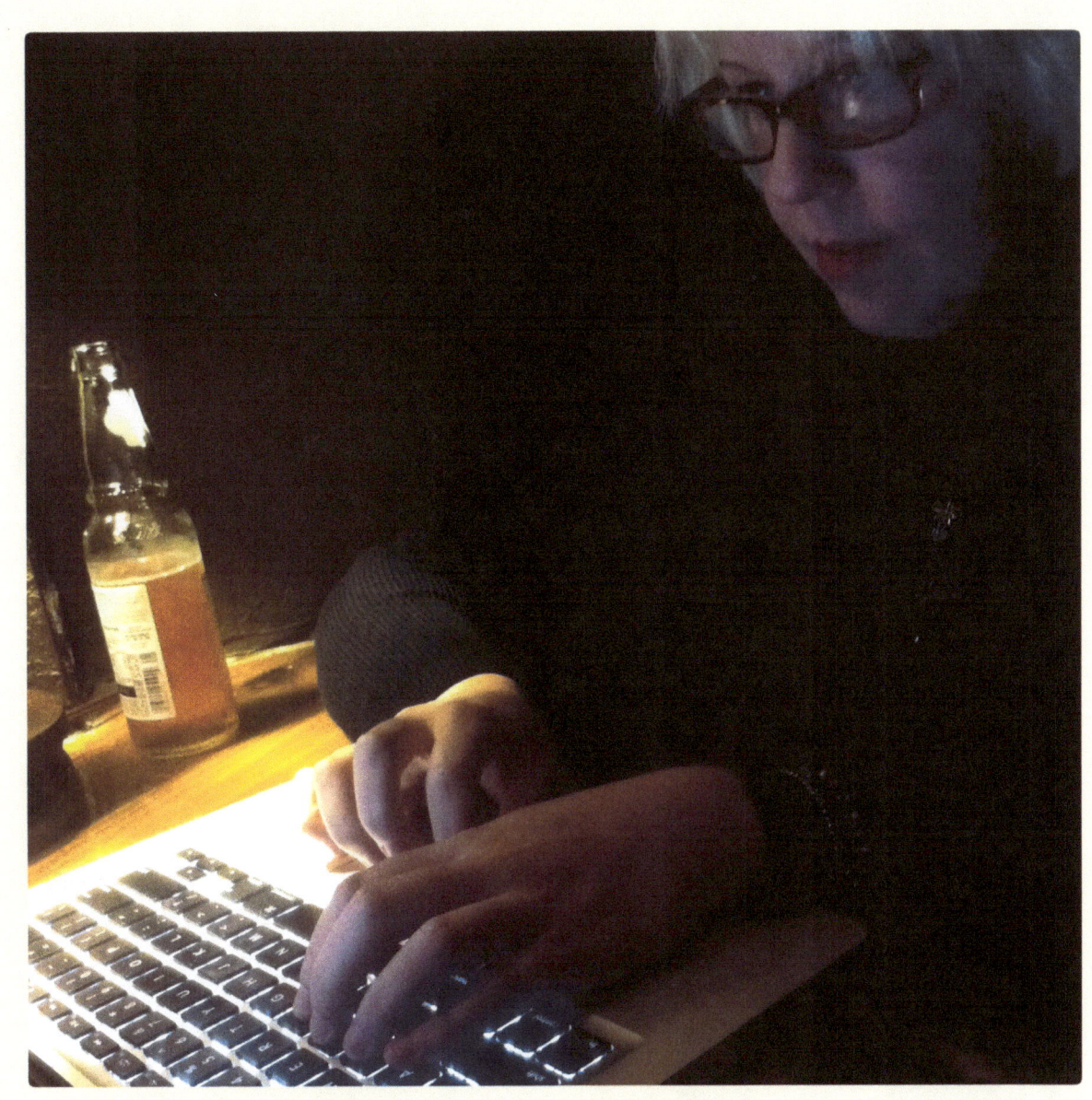

Hannah (Lil Indies)

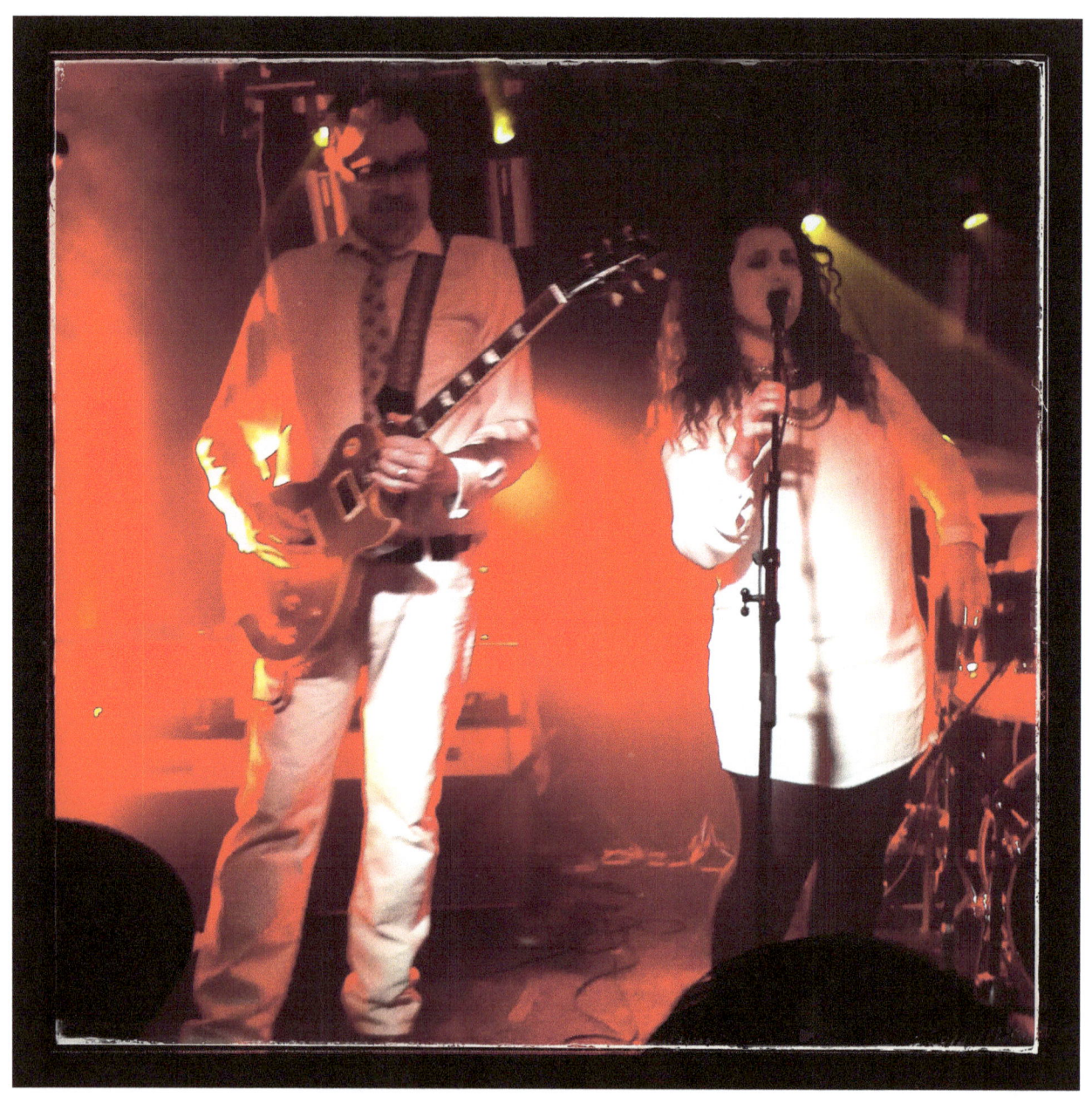

Jeff Nolan and Kaleigh Baker (Will's Pub)

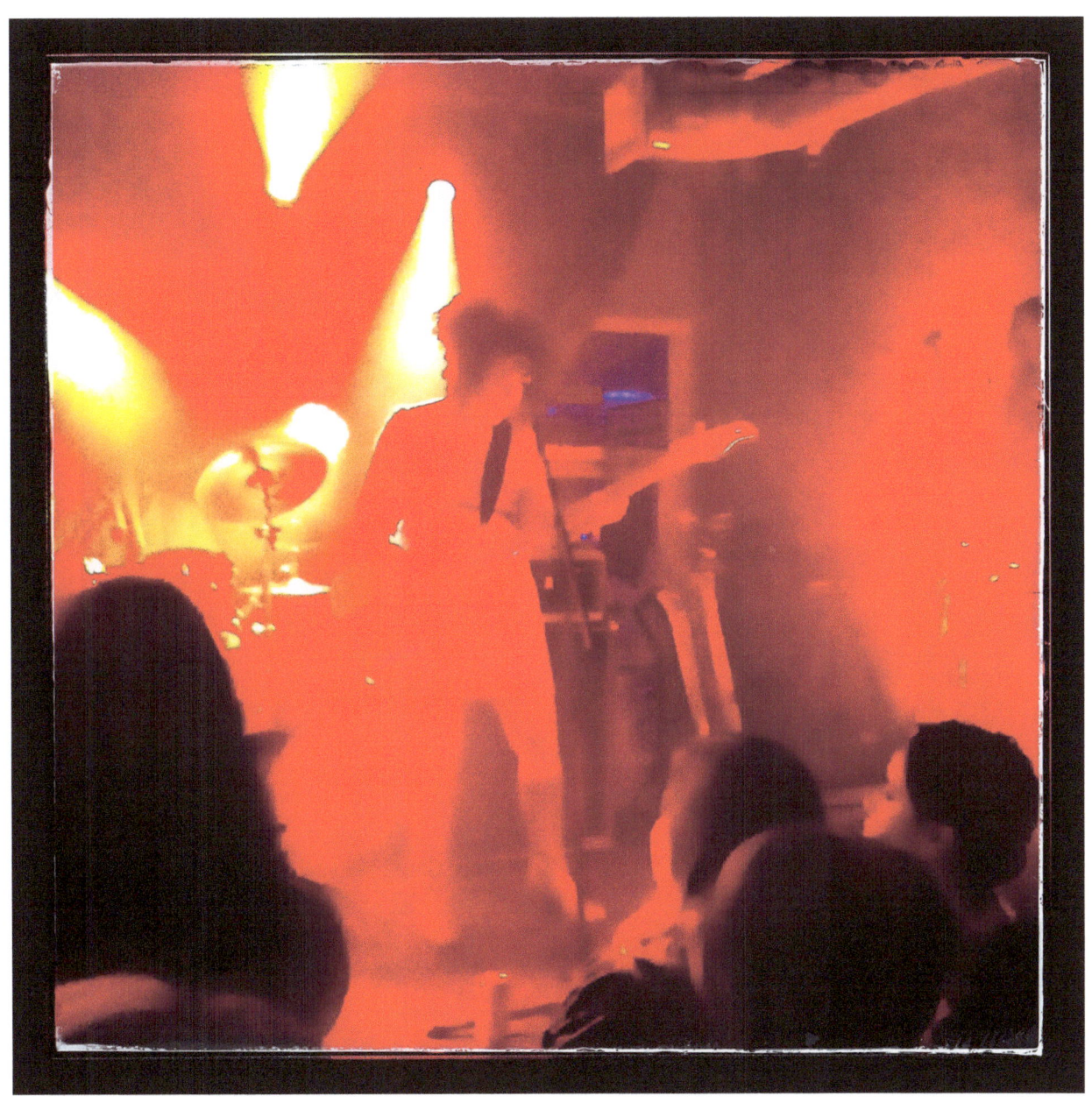

Erin Nolan (Will's Pub)

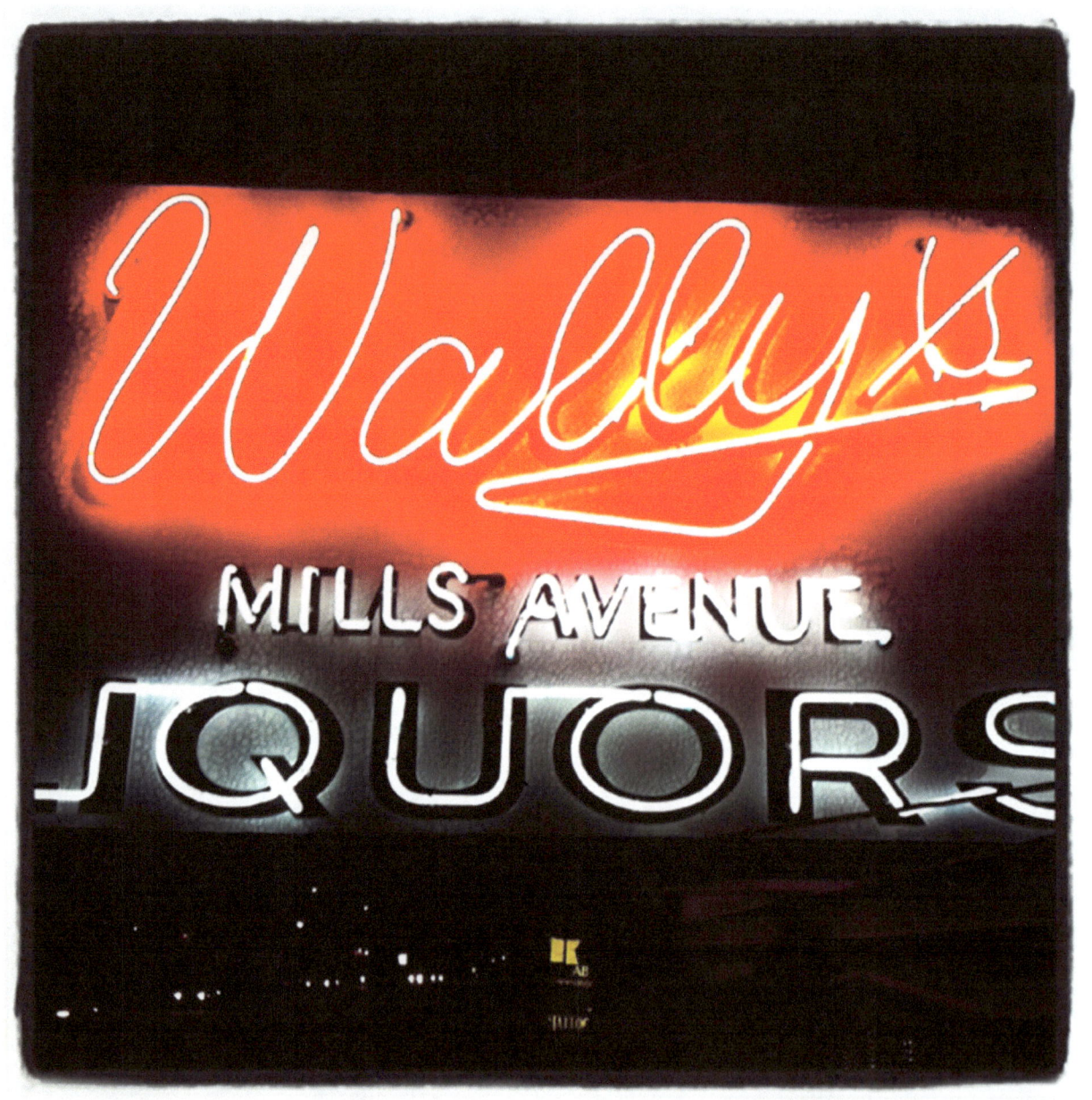

Wally's

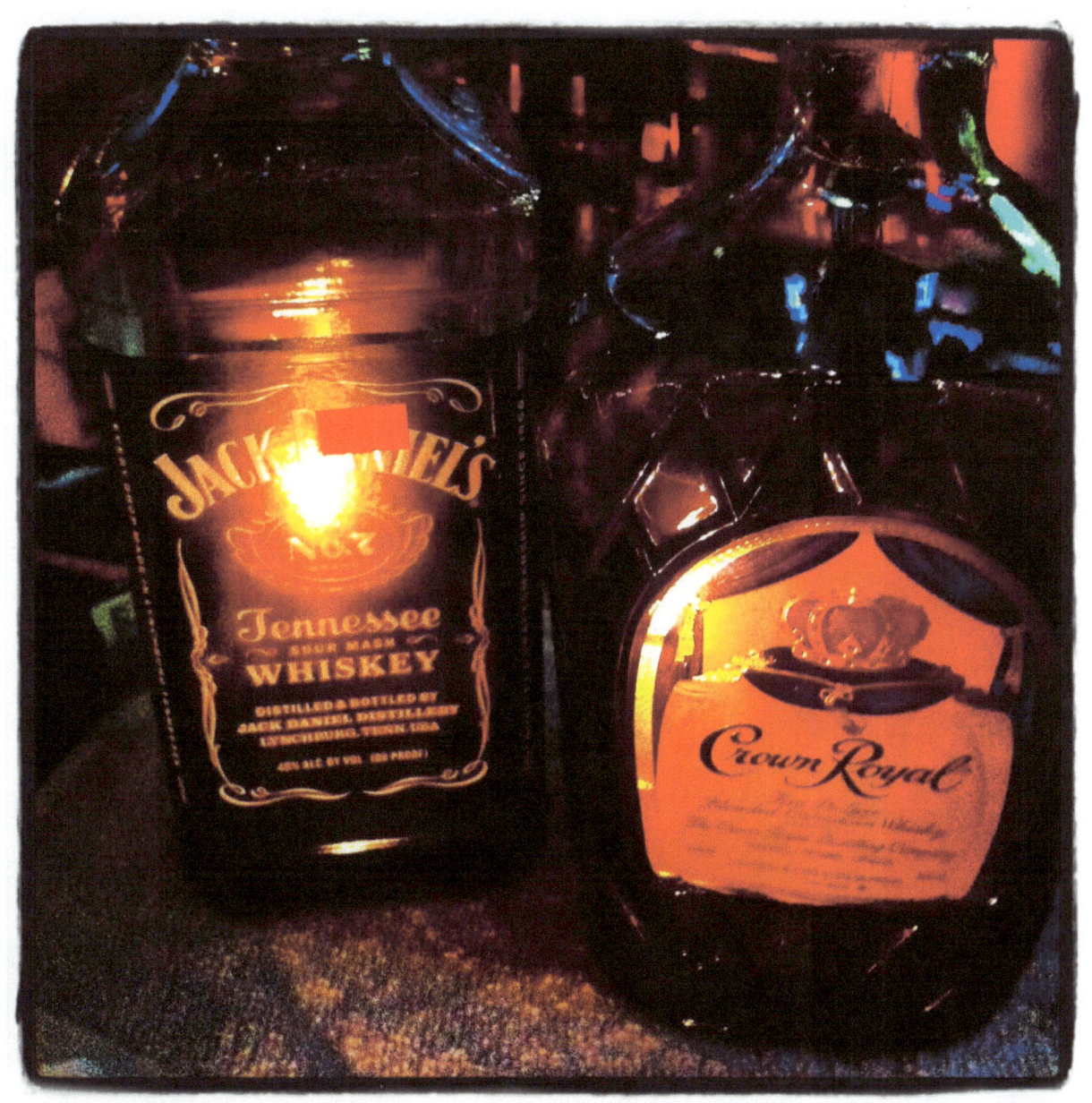

The Good Stuff (Wally's)

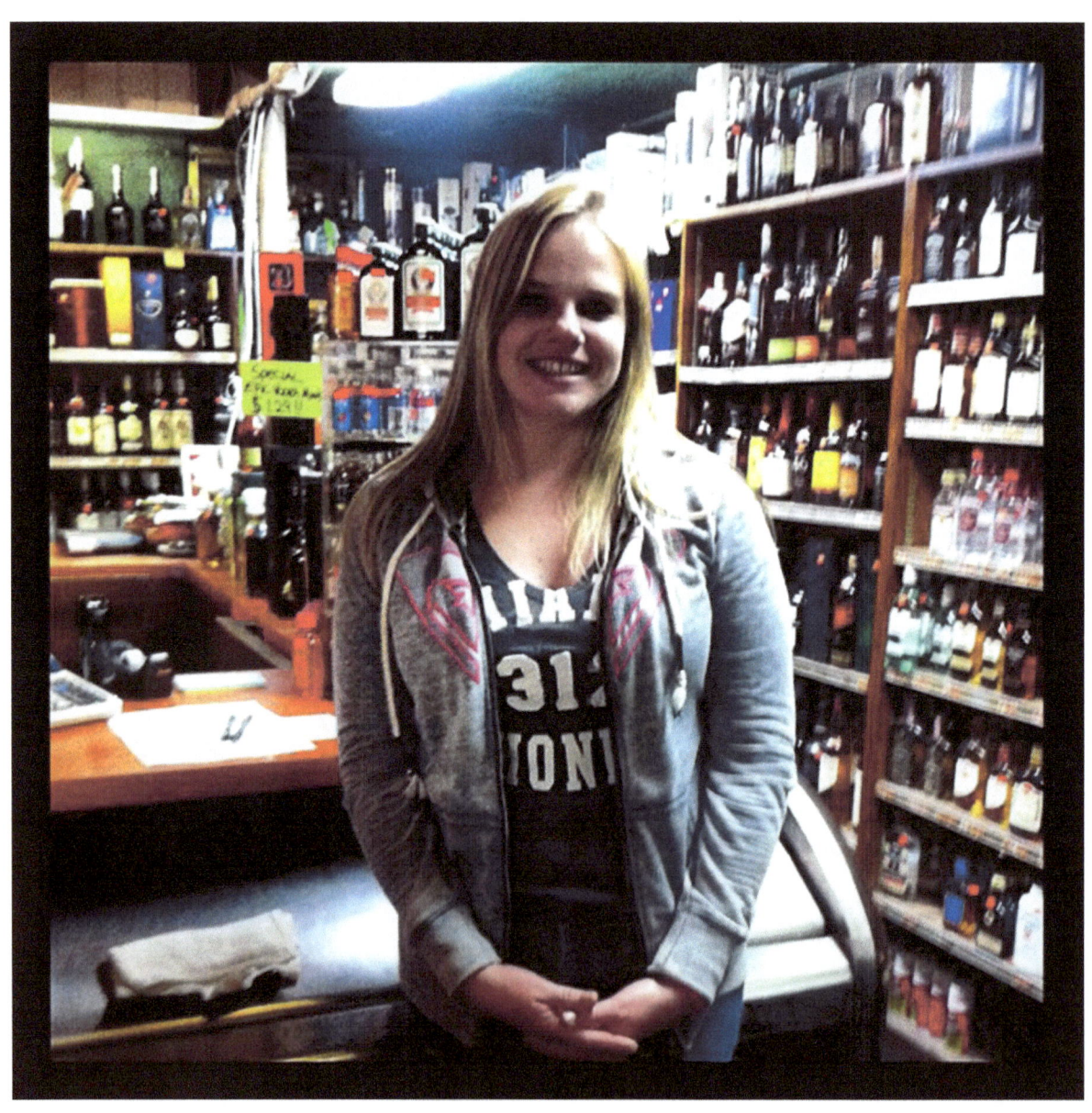

Jenna (Wally's)

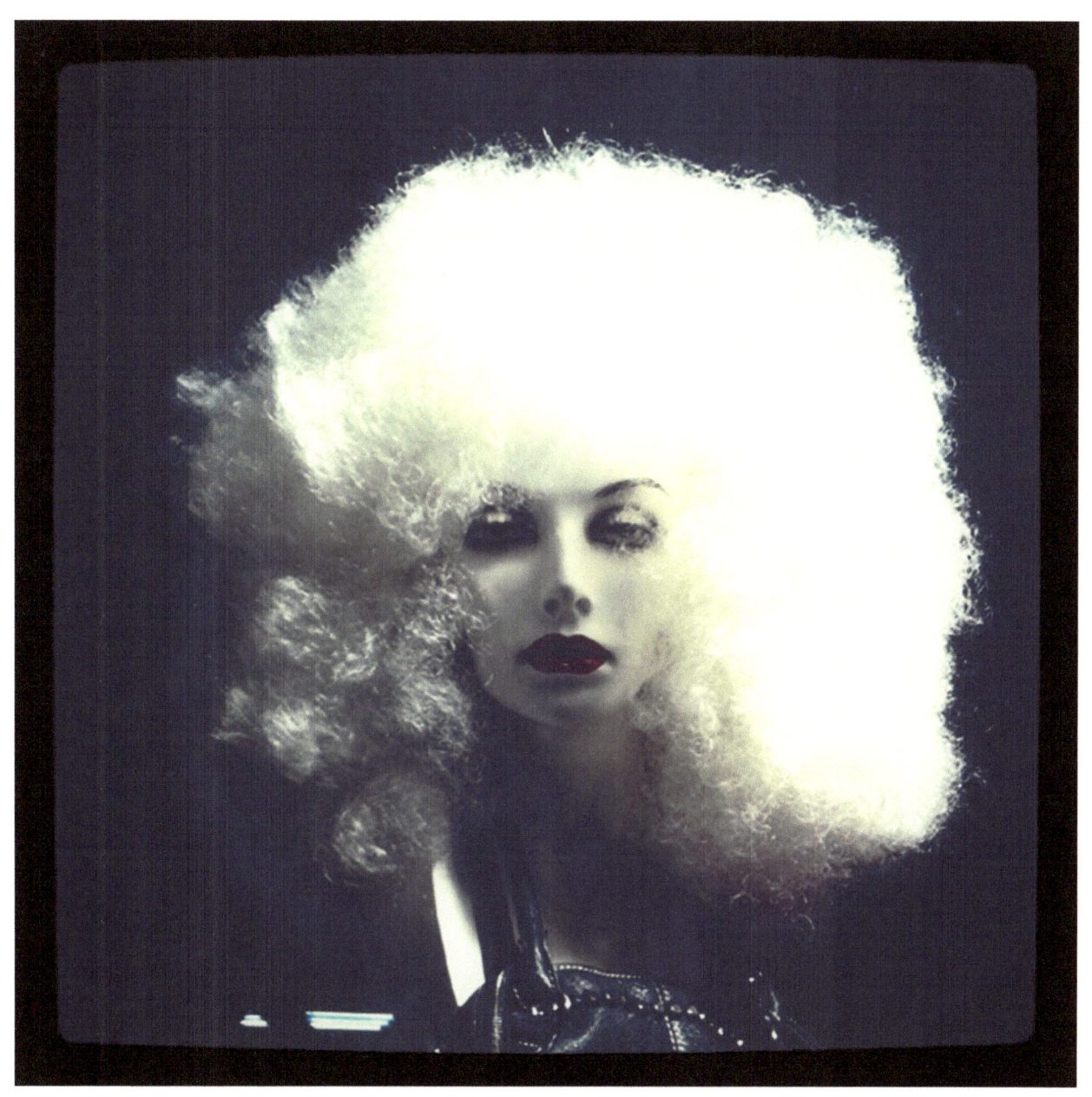

Window Display (Ritzy Rags)

7.
Miscellaneous Orlando, Florida

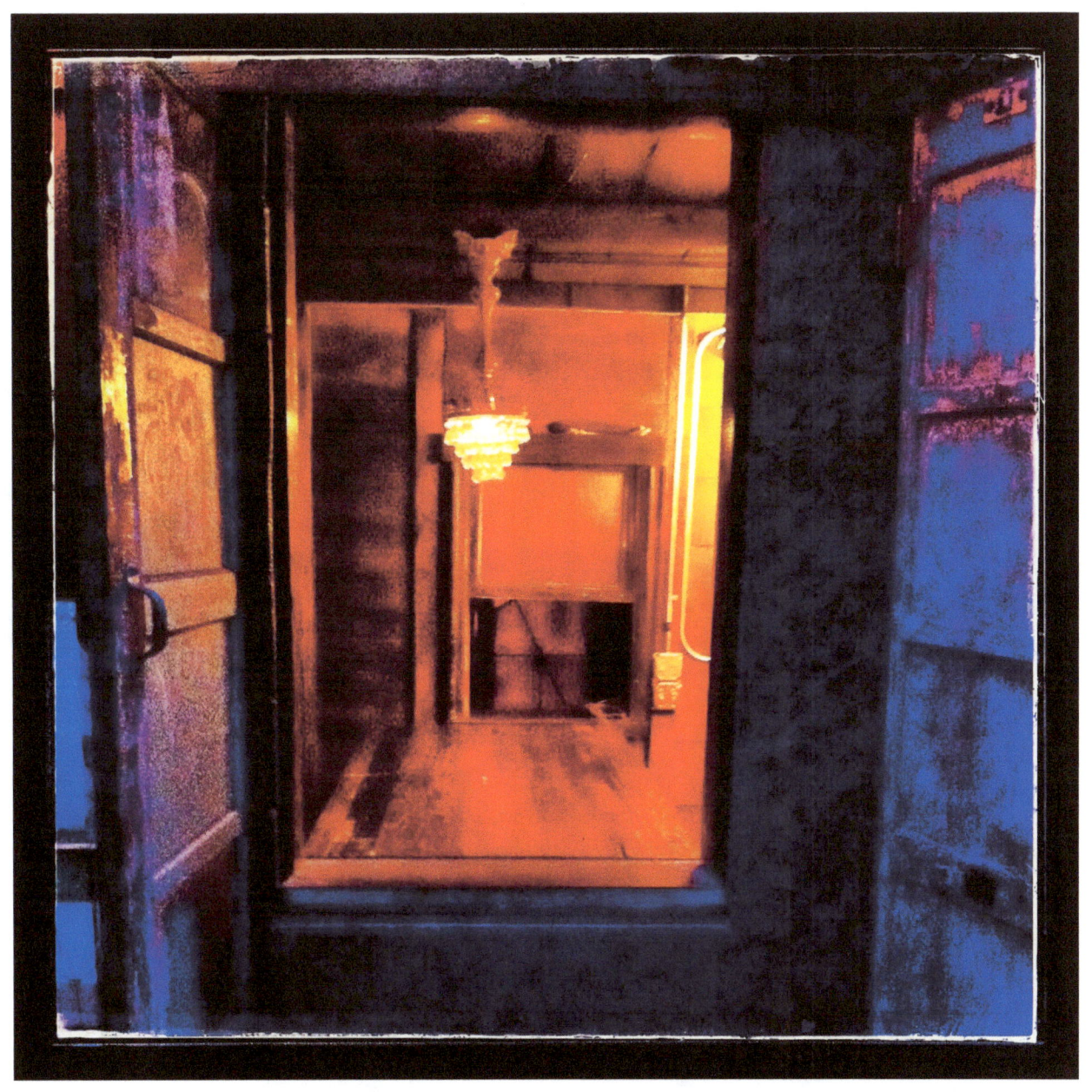

Window Leading to Bar, Sound Room and Dance Floor
(The Acre)

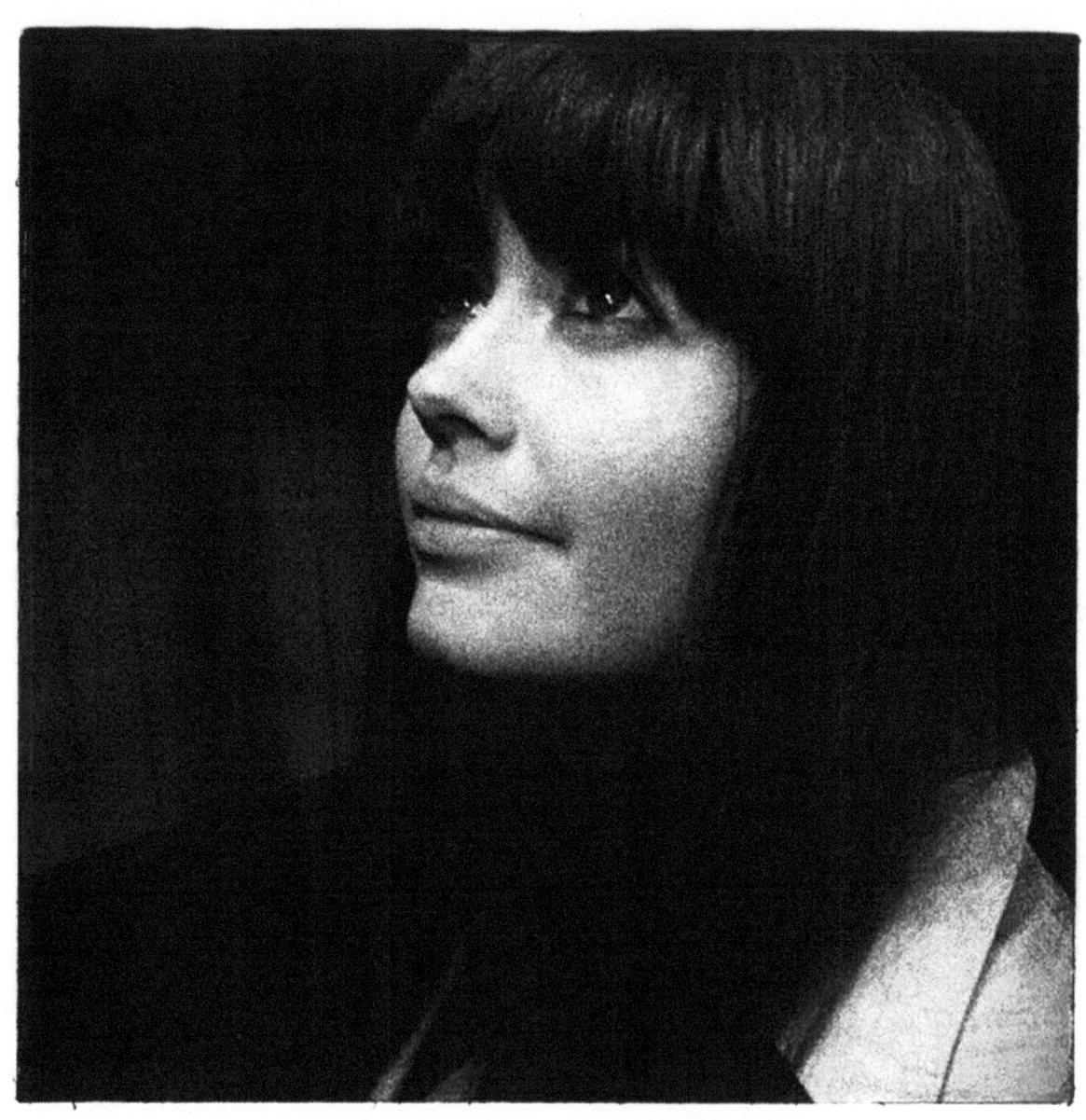

Bonnie Gardner (Friend's house)

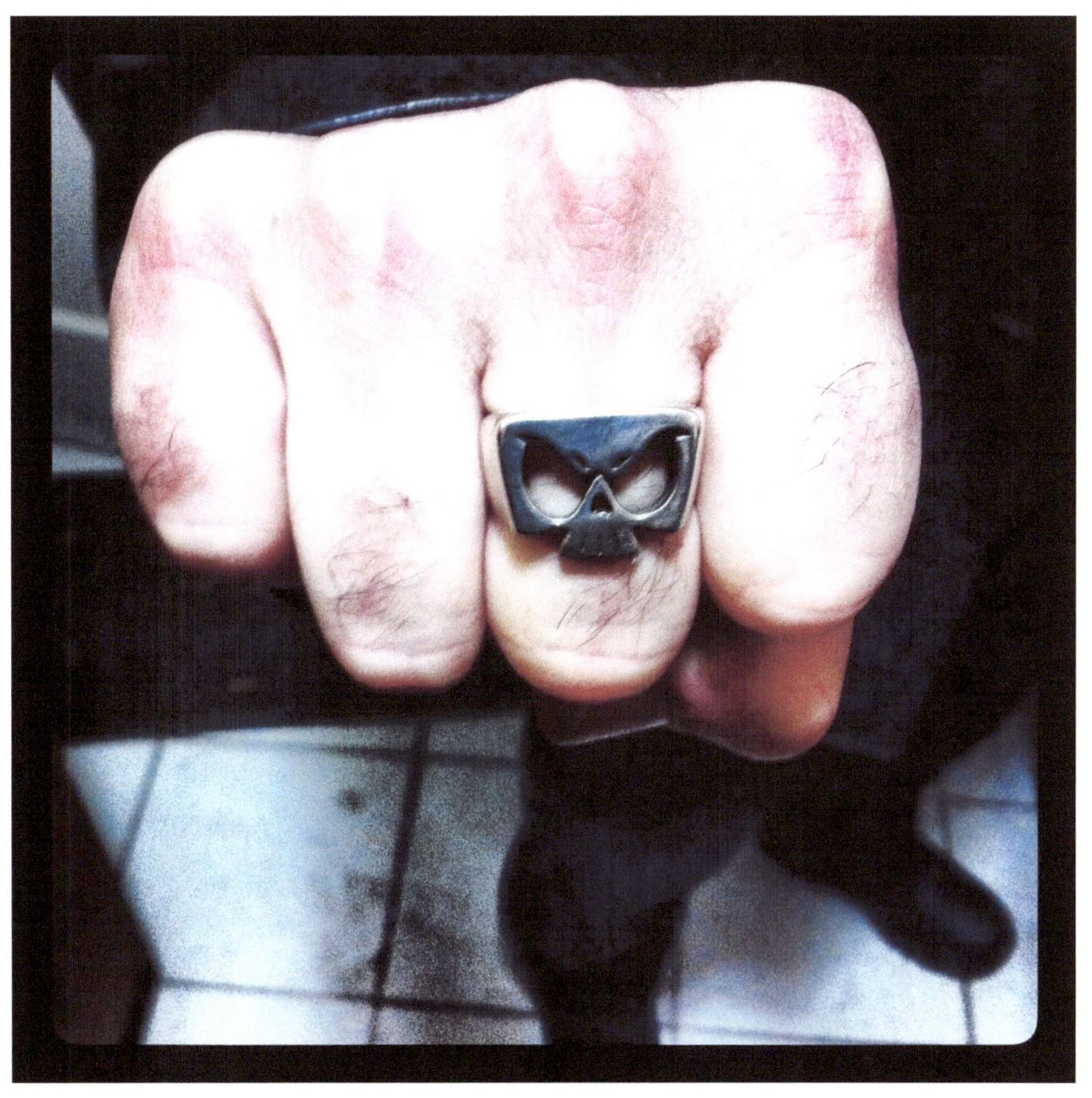

Brian Stibal and One of His Ring Creations
(Friend's house)

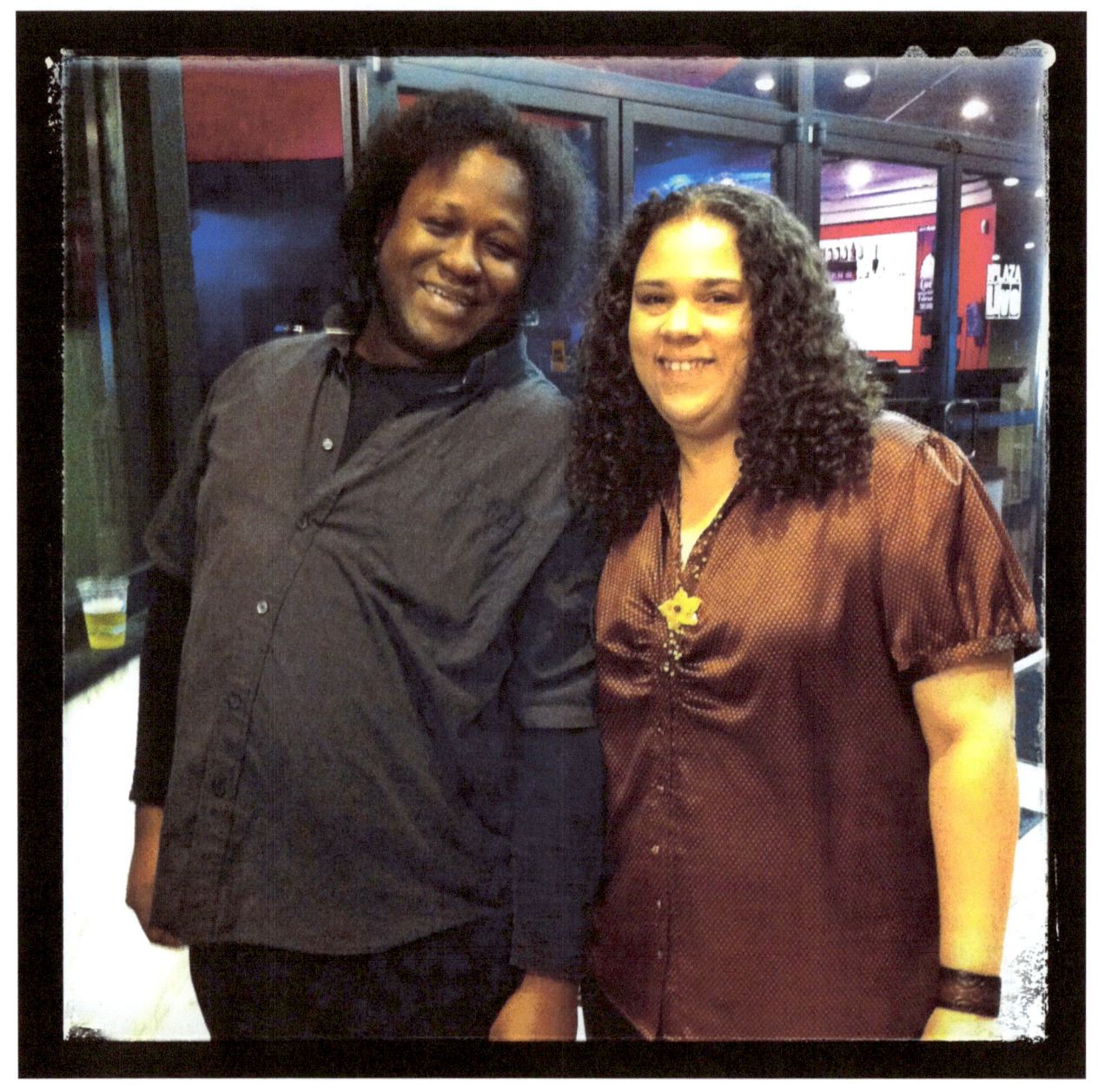

Multi-Instrumentalist Chris Lebrane and Companion
(The Plaza)

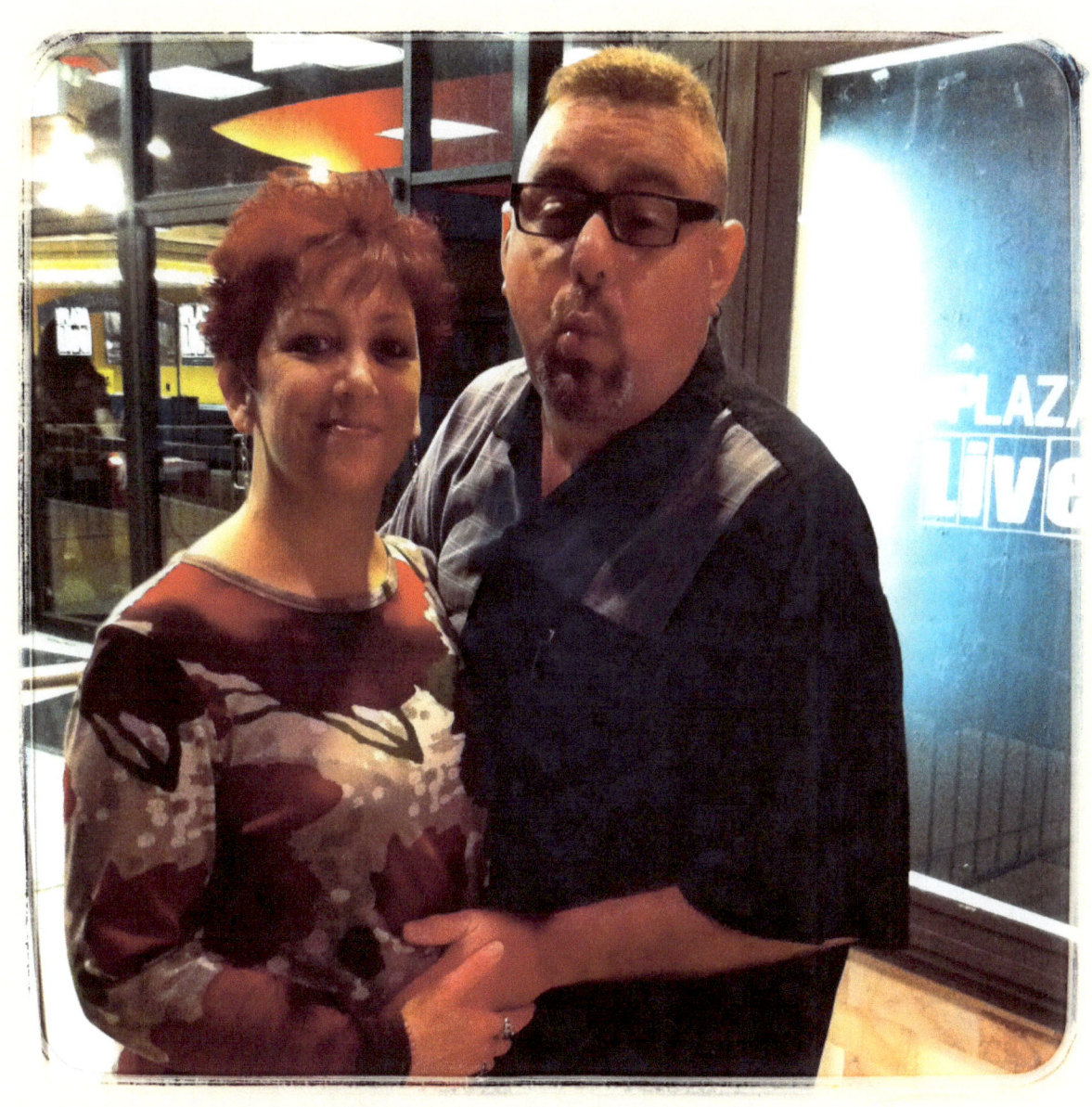

Jenny and Rich Miller (The Plaza)

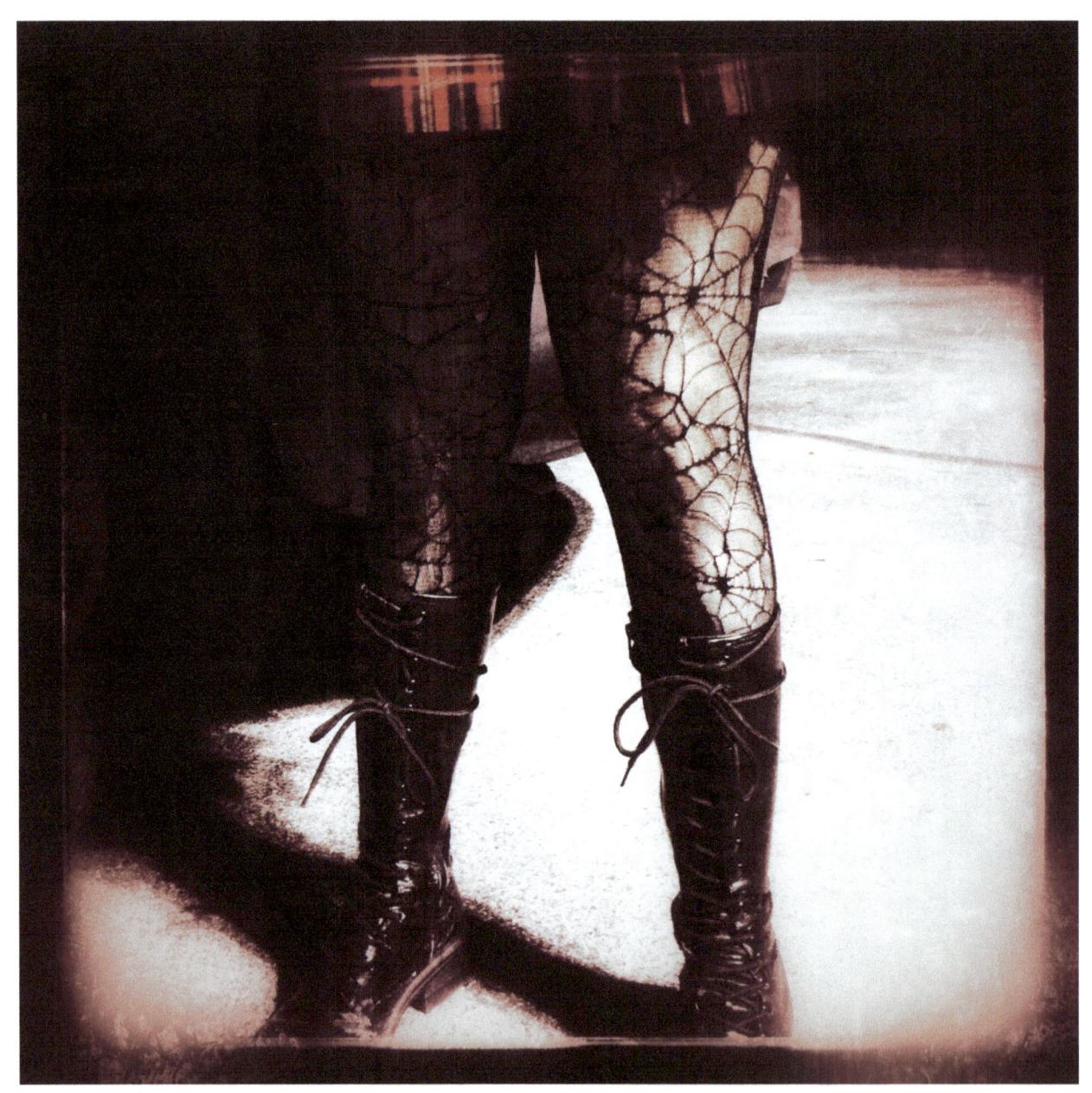

Denise Van Ness (The Plaza)

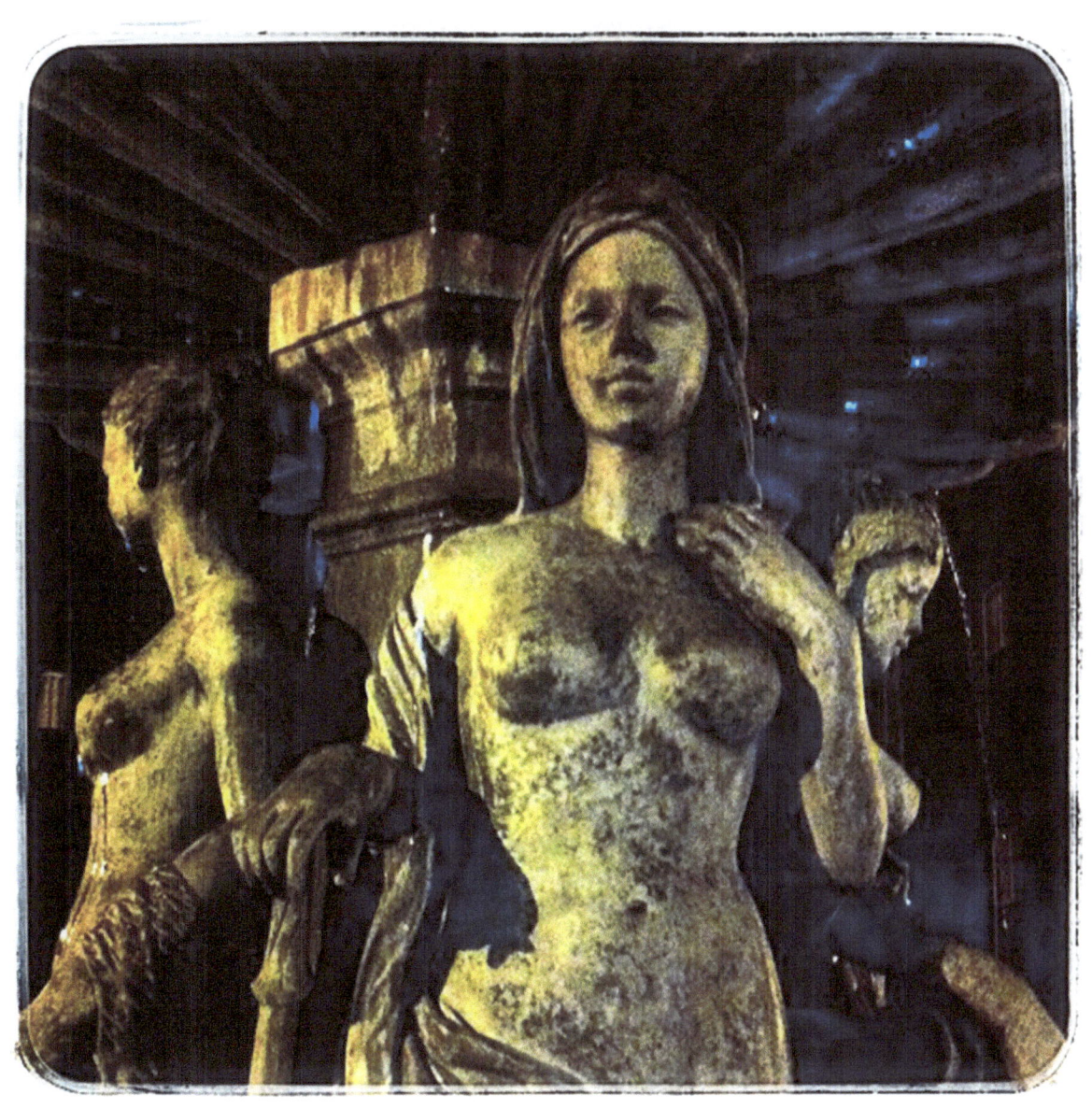

Thornton Park

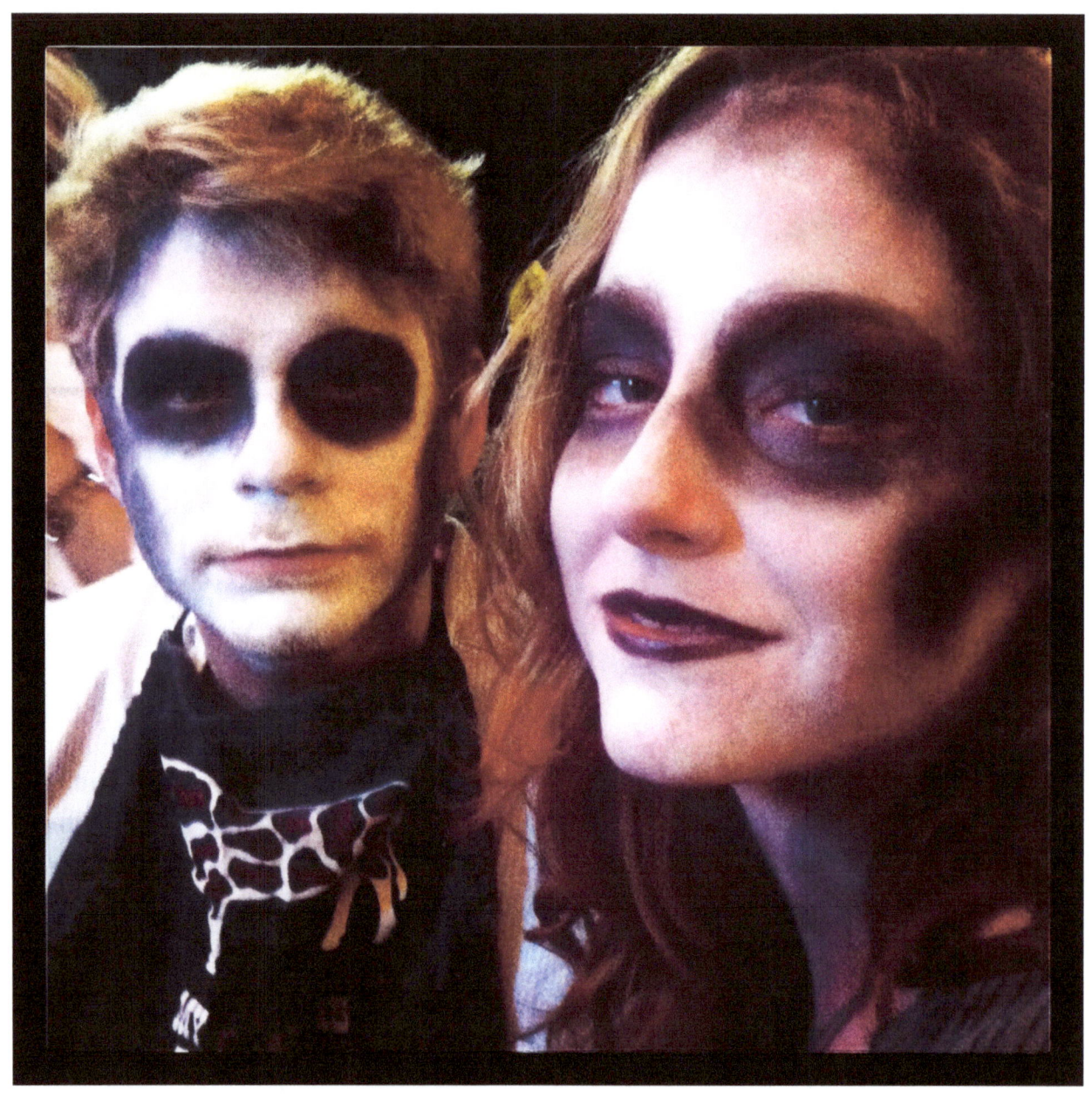

Heather Williams' Zombie Makeup
(The Falcon)

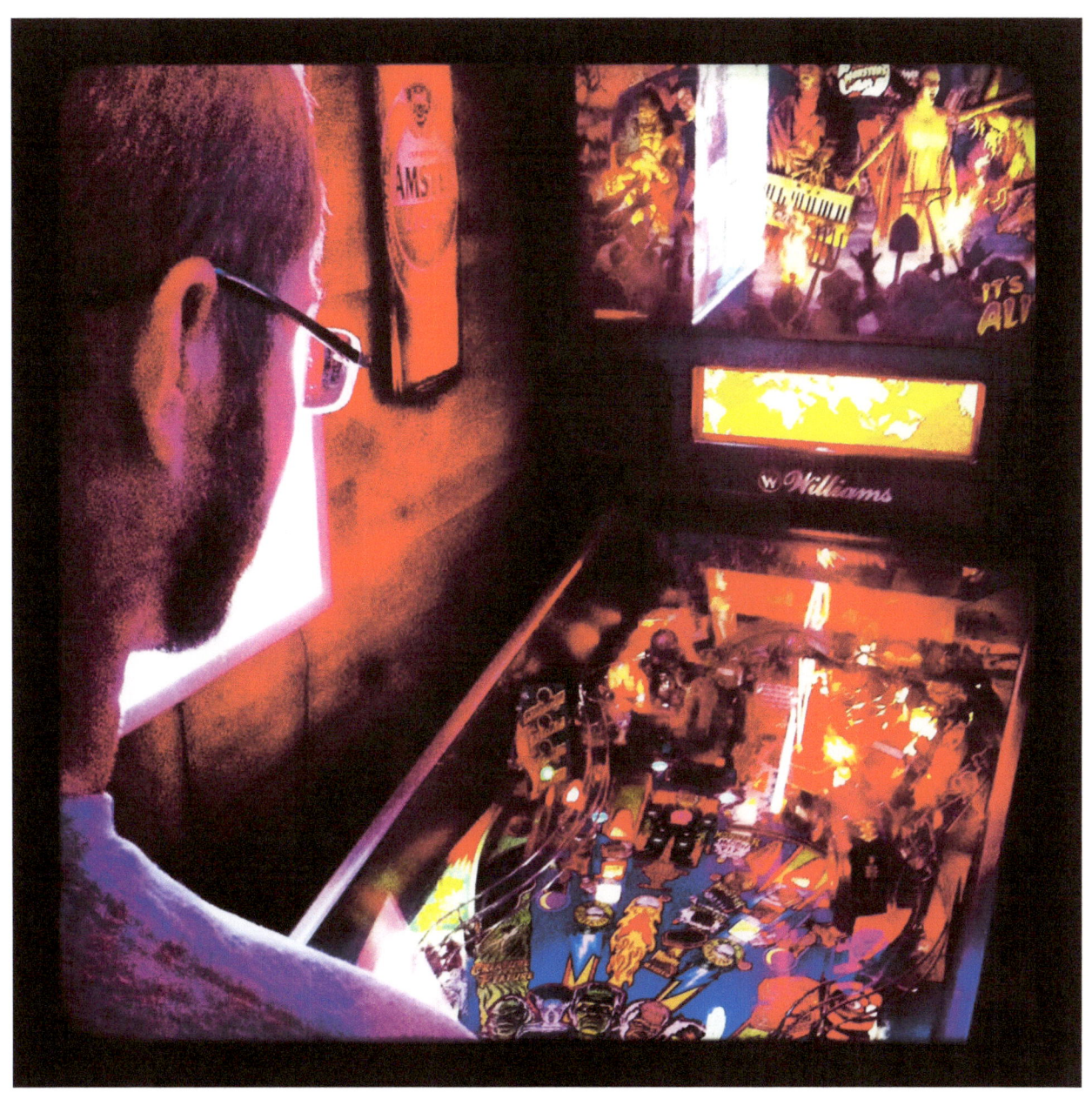

Casey Dayhoff (Hideaway Bar)

8.
Sanford, Florida

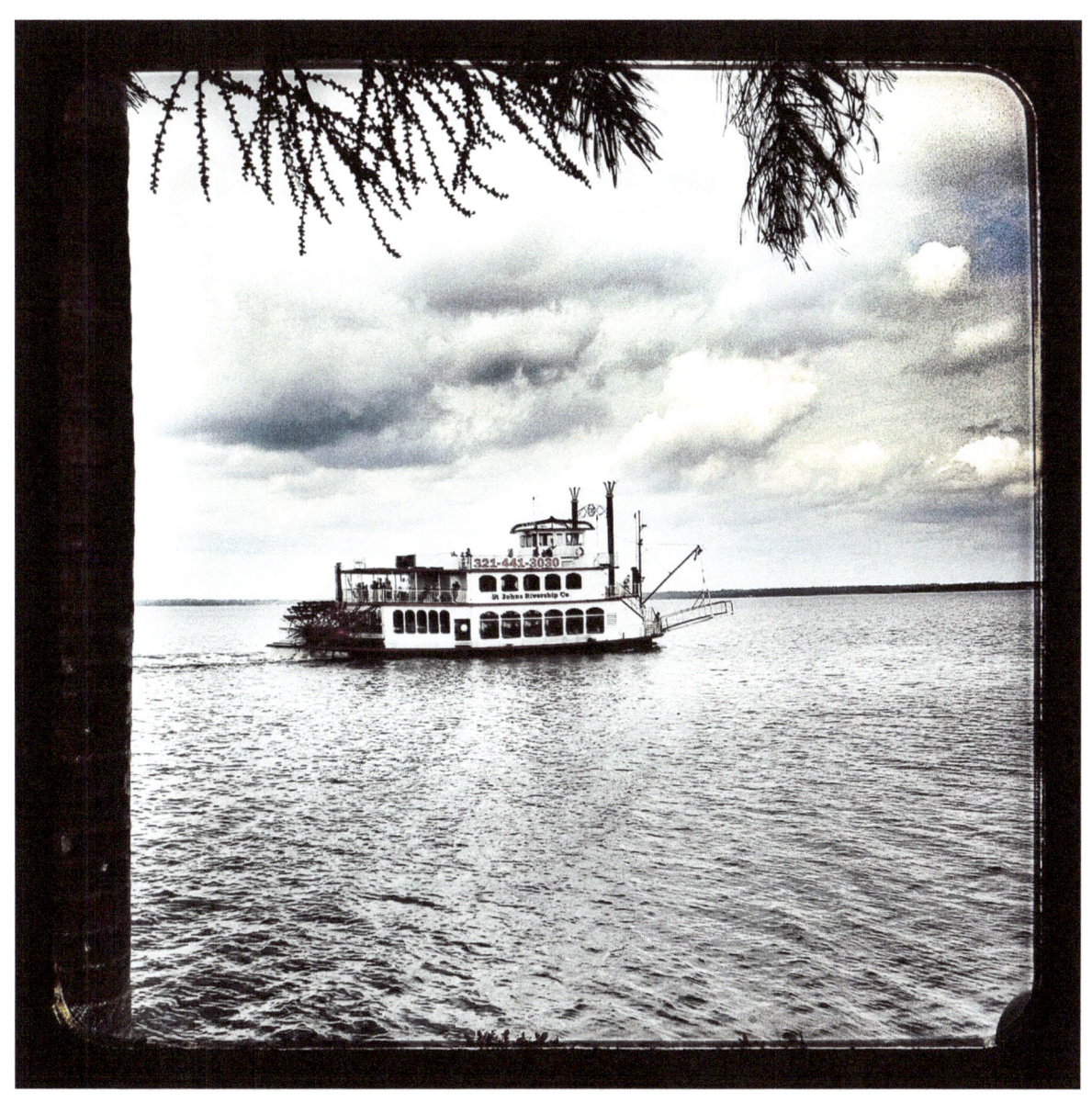

Rivership Barbara Lee Cruising Lake Monroe

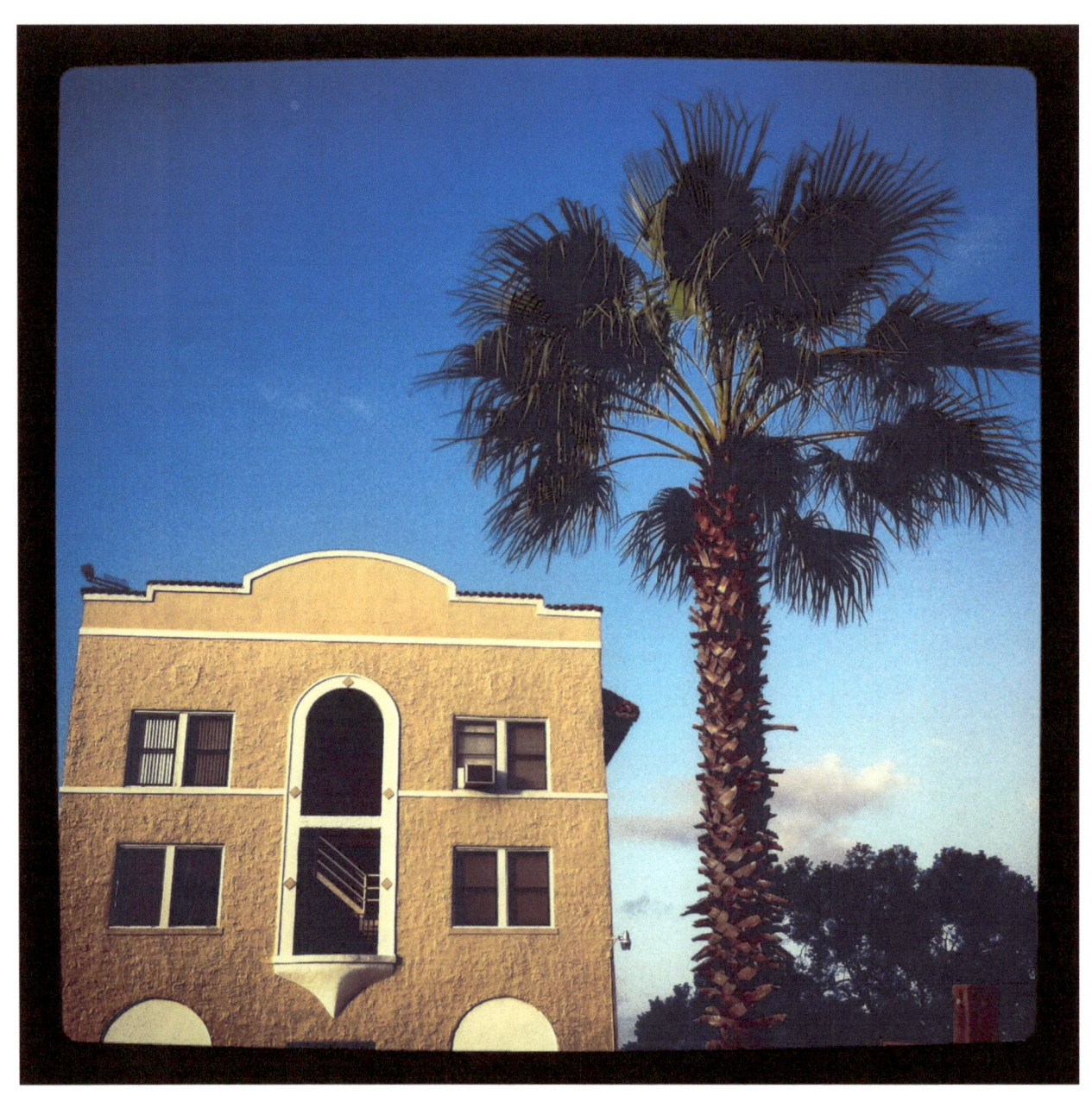

New Tribe Mission

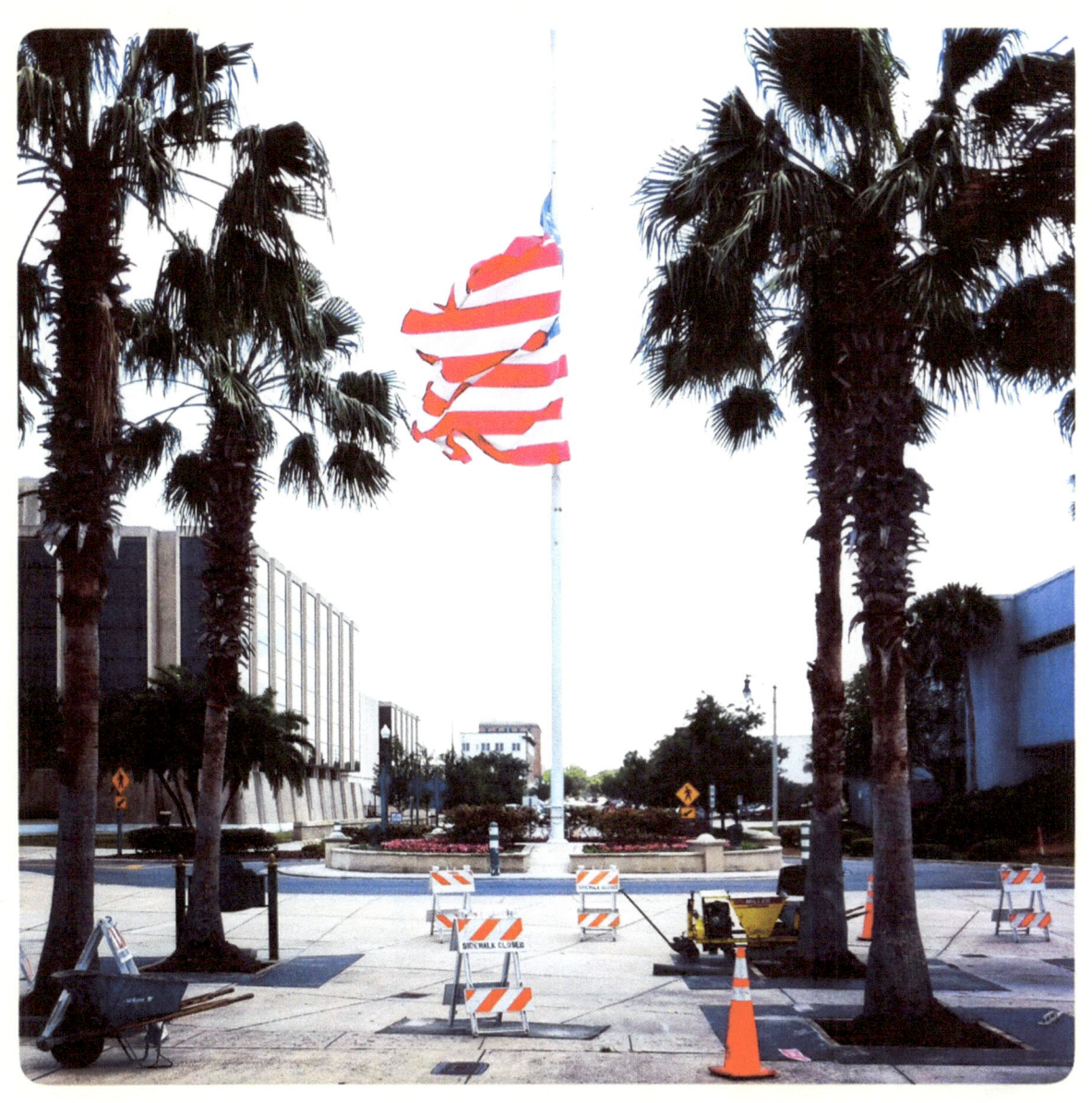

Half-Mast Honoring 2013 Boston Bombing Victims

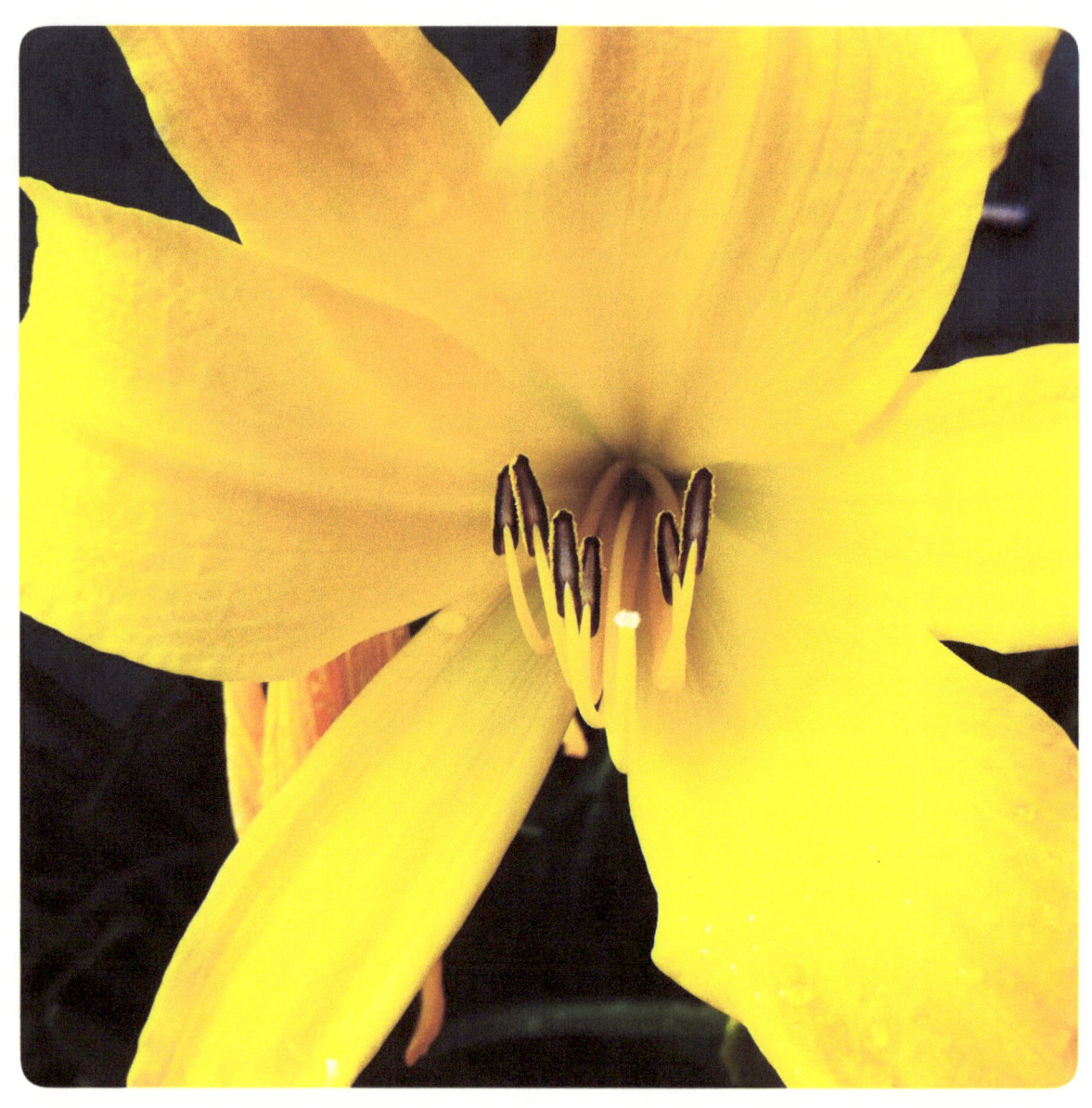

Day Lily (Grandma Eva's house)

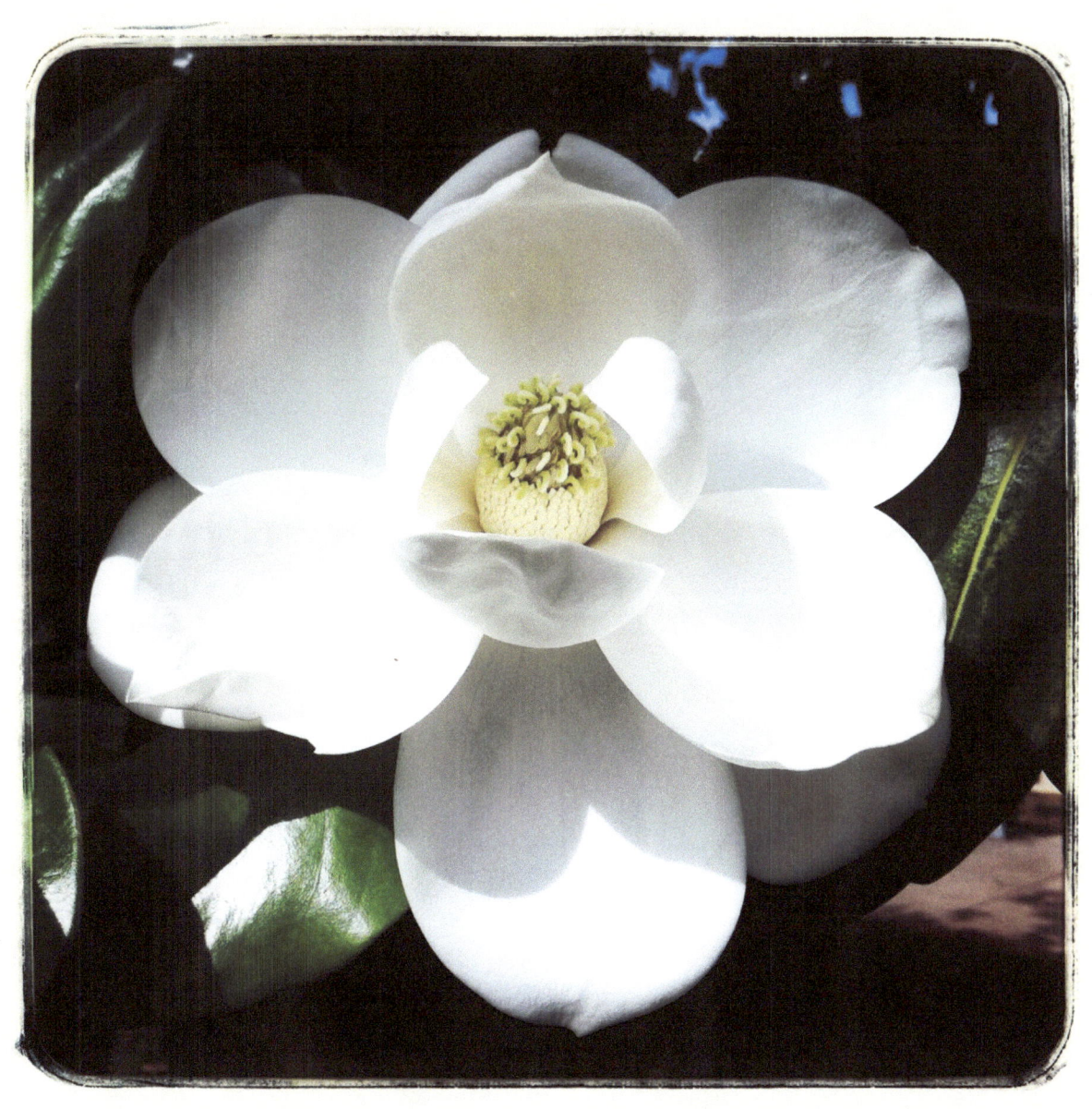

Southern Magnolia
(Corner of 1st and Sanford Ave.)

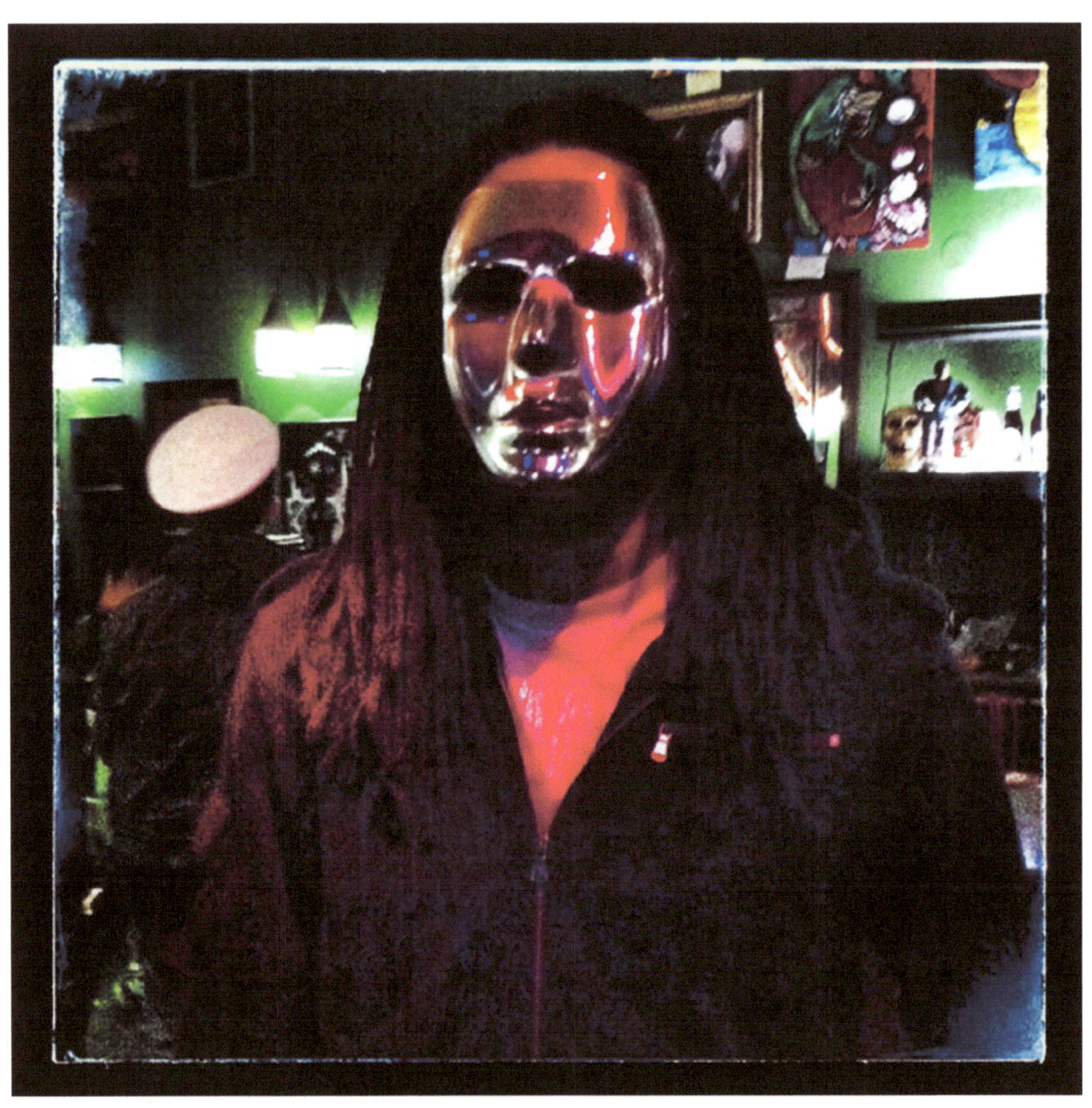

Masked, Dreadlock Guy (Little Fish, Huge Pond)

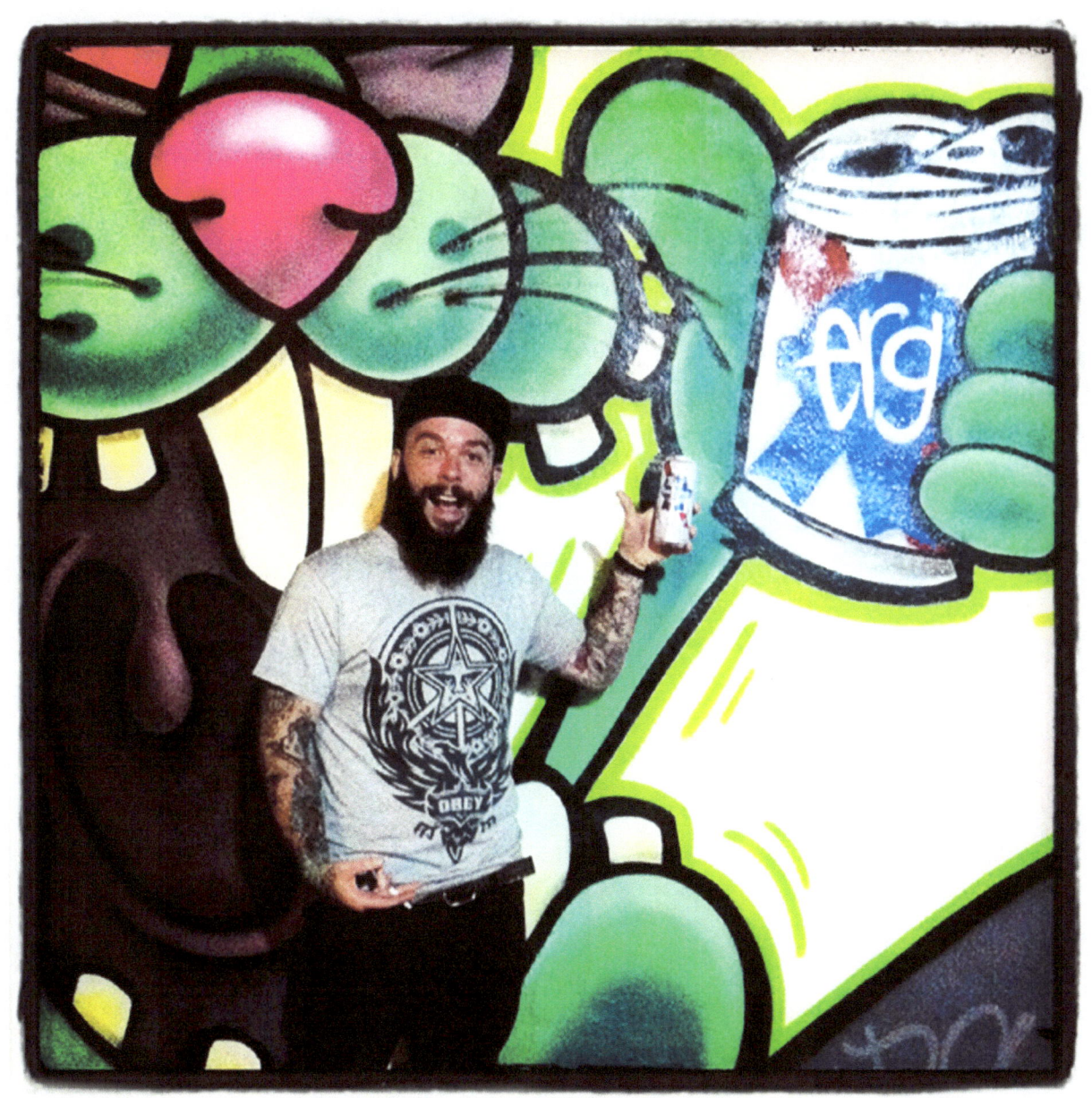

Graffiti Artist Timmy Dub
(Ms. Pat's Fish and Wings)

About the Photographer

Born in Sanford, Patrick Scott Barnes is an events photographer. Occasionally, he does weddings.

Besides photography, Central Florida mostly knows him for spoken-word. Patrick Scott Barnes also DJs.

His Instagram name is Stonecrazy89.

www.ingramcontent.com/pod-product-compliance
Lightning Source LLC
Chambersburg PA
CBHW050744180526
45159CB00003B/1341